474 THIRD STREET
PARK SLOPE
BROOKLYN

ROBIN VIVERITO KAPPLER

474 THIRD STREET, PARK SLOPE, BROOKLYN

Acknowledgements

I want to thank my son, **Christopher Jon Kappler:**
Each time I thought I wouldn't be able to master
the graphics, the table of contents, or the ability to send a
finished copy to the publisher, I would receive an invitation
to share screens on zoom. Chris' face would appear,
and he would pull me through, into his house
where we would solve the problems.

I also want to acknowledge my cousins,
Patty Leigy and **Joann Viverito May,** for preserving
so much information I was able to use
in the writing of these stories.

Special thanks to my granddaughter **Annika Kappler**
for her sketch of 474 Third Street, and to my husband,
Gustav Edward Kappler, for his artistic ability with photos.

TABLE OF CONTENTS

Prologue

CHAPTER 1

1899 · Sicily to America

Life in Sicily for a young woman was not easy. Girls were expected to stay at home and help clean and cook. The daughters cared for the younger children. Women could do very little outside the home. Most Sicilians were conservative and suspicious, and parents oversaw daughters.

I must invent Josephine from my research about Sicily. Chances are she had long black hair. I see her with it pulled back and lots of curls escaping around her face. She had a solid ethnic Italian look, and she wore her clothing loose to hide her generous figure. Had she been less modest, she might have shown a curvy body, an Italian woman's figure, with her tiny waist. We don't know whether Josephine met Crescenzo on her own and fell in love or whether it was an arranged marriage. By the time their oldest child was ten, they decided that life in Sicily would never be what they had hoped. Jobs were difficult to get, and patronage and nepotism were prevalent. The mafia was entrenched.

There is some discrepancy in his birth year in the records I found. Charles D. and Carlos D. were both used for him. His name was Crescenzo Vivirito, and the officers at Ellis Island changed it to Viverito. We have no idea what the D stands for. Some records state that he was born in 1862, and others state 1873, and there is similar information about Josephine. I choose to use the dates from their local church in the Parish of Tribia, Archdiocese of Palermo. On February 5, 1894, Josephine married Crescenzo in the Sanctuary of the Madonna of Melicia. The church records say that Crescenzo was born in 1873. He lived for 66 years. His parents were Joseph and Gaetana Arcana Viverito. Josephine's parents were Giovanni Batista and Angela Randazzo Damiano.

The crossing was long and difficult. The young couple arrived in America with their three children, Joseph, Gertrude, and Helen. The young family was greeted by older cousins with whom they stayed for a few weeks while looking for their own home. The family entered America through Ellis Island. Thanks to the kindness of his granddaughter, Patti Liegy, you can find the name Joseph A. Viverito listed on the wall of Ellis Island today.

They lived on Third Street in Brooklyn, close to other family members until 1940. I also lived on Third Street. When Josephine died, Crescenzo had long since returned to Sicily and was buried there. Even though he had fulfilled his dream to become a citizen of the United States, he returned to his roots.

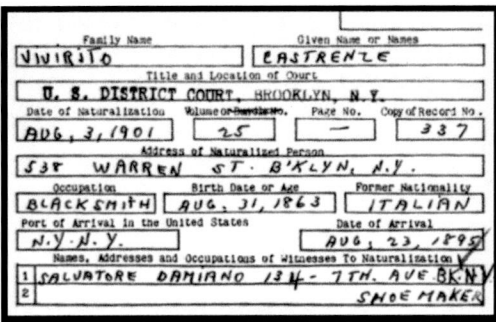

Josephine died in early 1940s, a few weeks before I was born. She is buried in Brooklyn.

CHAPTER 2

1910 · Saint Josephine

Children were spilling out the doors and windows of the brownstone on the corner of Third Street and Seventh Avenue in Brooklyn in 1899. Inside, the tomato sauce was simmering on the stove, blending with the clean smell of freshly ironed clothes. Josephine took in washing and ironing to earn extra dollars for her children. Gertrude, Helen, and Anita helped by caring for the two youngest boys, Frank and John.

Joseph, the oldest child, was the star. Tall and slim, he was good at all sports and kept an impressive grade point average. He was born in Sicily and spoke fluent Italian, acting as a translator for his parents.

According to stories, this woman, the grandmother I never knew, was a saint who raised six children during difficult times. Born Josephine Damiano and married in a small church in Alta Villa Melicia, Sicily, to Crescendo Viverito, Josephine did not have an easy life. My grandfather was a blacksmith in Sicily, not far from Palermo. Alta Villa is built on a cliff above the blue sea. Leaving their home, as did many Italian immigrants looking for a better life, the Viveritos sailed to America in 1899. My grandfather was skilled in metal, and he went to work for the railroad.

Joseph and Gertrude were in school and learning English very quickly, speaking with no accent. During the years, five more children were born. They were a happy family.

This way of life came to a screeching halt when two railroad cars joined too quickly, and Crescendo was caught between, losing his right leg. After that, he became depressed and verbally abusive at home, banging the dinner table with his fist and yelling, *"Silencio."*

I broke my ankle in high school and was given a walking cast; Daddy said, "I get nervous when I hear you coming. I think my father is coming; his walk with his wooden leg sounded exactly like yours." Our older families did not pass on stories of their immigrant parents or their young lives. This was the first story I ever heard about anything about my grandfather.

He received a small settlement. The railroad lawyers took advantage of his lack of English. And he never went back to work. Eventually, he returned to Sicily, leaving Josephine and the six children to fend for themselves. The older children had jobs, and they managed. Joseph was in dental school, and soon he would help support the entire family. Despite all this, my father remembered a happy childhood. His three older sisters spoiled him. I could see their love for him. Uncle John did tell us he remembered Aunt Anita sitting him up on the bureau to dress him.

Daddy had a scar on the side of his cheek. The story is that Gertrude, Helen, and Anita were making taffy. He asked to taste it and was told it was too hot, but he grabbed some and ran. It stuck to his cheek, and Francesco would not come out from under the bed. By the time they coaxed him out, he had a burn.

All the children attended Saint Saviour's School on Sixth Street and Eighth Avenue. A lifetime later, when I was a student at the same school, a few nuns had taught my father when they were young teachers. They were very fond of him and were incredibly friendly to us.

Uncle Joe, the oldest, was always referred to as "Our Brother Joe." He took over as head of the household, and the five brothers and sisters revered him.

As a high school student at Manual Training three blocks away, my father made a group of friends who were to last him through adulthood. He played tight end on the football team. Later, Uncle John had a car, and there was no lack of pretty girls stuffed into the old Ford. Daddy was a techie before the word was coined. He fixed the steering wheel so that he or Uncle John could remove it and steer with a tiny inside wheel. When girls complained about their driving, he would hand them the steering wheel, saying, "Okay, you can drive." Many crowd photos were taken in that car and at Coney Island. The boys' bathing suits were one-piece sleeveless affairs.

In many other photos taken at the park, the young men wear three-piece suits and fedoras. The girls are all wearing clingy dresses popular in the twenties with high heels—and what else? Hats!

Dad was accepted to Georgia Tech; had he gone, all our lives would have been different. "Our Brother Joe" intervened. He was now a dentist and decided that Frank should be a dental technician, working with him in his office. So, no college for Frank.

John had gone to NYU on the GI bill, becoming a Phys Ed teacher and swimming coach at Brooklyn Tech. Gertrude became a principal. She had a master's degree from NYU. Anita went to work for Abraham and Strauss, and Helen married a doctor. How they achieved this with no father present, and a mother who still spoke her native Sicilian Italian is a mystery to my sisters, my cousins, and me.

Maybe Josephine, who died three weeks after I was born, was a saint. At the very least, she was a powerful and brave woman I wish I had known. Following in Josphine's footsteps, two more generations of her descendants had families of three sisters.

 The photos below show Josephine's three daughters: Anita, Helen, and Gertrude Viverito. My father also had three daughters: Robin, Janet, and Muffin. The most recent generation, Katya, Sabrina, and Annika Kappler, are young women of whom she would be very proud.

As for me, I had a daughter and a son, and one grandson in addition to my three granddaughters above. I love the idea that we can all trace our lineage back to Josephine.

CHAPTER 3

1922 · Our Wild Irish Rose

Rose Irma Dolores McAvoy, my mother, had flashing green eyes and red hair. To my disappointment, I do not have a clear picture of her childhood.

As an adult, she was admired for her grace and charm. She always knew the correct behavior, the right gift to give, and wrote the perfectly phrased thank-you note. Her bearing was regal, and her clothing, all of which she made herself, quite sophisticated. She also made our clothing and dressed my two sisters and me alike. We had dresses with pinafores and hand-knitted sweaters in any style we loved. I wanted a majorette's sweater, and she even figured out how to make the epaulets. I wish I had a picture of me in that unique sweater because I loved it!

I only have a vague idea of my Mom's childhood. She was the youngest of six and had an indulgent father and a very strict and unkind mother. They lived in a brownstone on Eighth Avenue across from Prospect Park in Brooklyn.

Two of her brothers, Edward and Robert, died from tuberculosis, which was sweeping the country in the 1930s.

Later, when the parents died, Uncle Tommy was considered the head of the family and a wonderful man. The youngest, Uncle Kenny, a sailor in the Navy, provided us with five redheaded, freckle-faced cousins, and then he disappeared forever.

Mom had one sister, Eileen, a scary number. My five-year-old sister avoided her, and when my Mom asked her why, she said, "She looks me a look like I should die!" That about sums up Eileen, who always wore black and resembled Morticia from the Addams Family. She ordered us to call her "Eileen". She said, "Ants were insects that crawled on the ground."

Eileen graduated from FIT (Fashion Institute of Technology), which explains my mother's high-style designer look. I remember that Eileen got Mom a job as a Powers Model. Finding the John Powers Agency online, I read the following: *"Fame and fortune have come to many personalities trained in the methods originated by Mr. Powers. First Lady Jacqueline Kennedy, Raquel Welch, and Princess Grace of Monaco were all Powers Models. Jennifer Jones, Ava Gardner, Barbara Stanwyck, Lucille Ball, Lee Remick, Ann Margaret, Henry Fonda, and Tyrone Power were also models, working with the original John Robert Powers Agency in New York City. It was the premier agency from the 1920s through the 1940s."*

We did not know about John Robert Powers then, but it explains a great deal about my mother's self-confidence and her sense of drama. "My father owned a fleet of limousines, and I was driven to school each day," she told us. Later we learned that his business was a limo service in Manhattan, and they were well known, although she led us to believe it was for their private use.

We were horrified when she told us that her mother had an Irish temper. In her own words: "My mother would chase me around the dining room table with a belt." This woman was a grandmother I never knew and certainly never missed. Our mother didn't have to hit us because she could give a look that could stop you in your tracks!

We always lived in an apartment and never had a dining room, so I pictured this elegant home with massive garages full of limousines. I guess the sense of drama got passed on to my imagination.

Sarah Hawes McAvoy, the mom, is a grandmother we did not know. She was an excellent cook and passed this on to my mother. We had lovely dinners when I was growing up.

Mom went to Evander Childs High School, and my father went to Manual Training High School. I have no idea how they met, but they were terrific dancers. They often put on records inside a tall mahogany cabinet with a red velvet lining. There was a curved arm that held the needle. You had to be very careful when placing the needle on the record so you would not scratch its grooves.

We moved from Brooklyn when I was a freshman in high school, leaving our entire way of life behind. It surprised me that we moved seamlessly to public school and riding the school bus. We had always gone to Catholic school. We walked everywhere we wanted to go. We visited friends often and called to ask if we could stay for dinner. None of this was possible anymore. The schools were far, and Mommy didn't drive. There were no sidewalks, no movie theatres or stores of any kind.

Then we discovered that school would be our salvation. There were buses for everything. They took us to football games and the dances on nights following a home game. We ran for class offices and won. We played every intermural sport, keeping us after school every day. The late bus took us home where a dinner plate would be on top of a steaming pot and covered with aluminum foil.

During the summer, Mom created teenage dances at the Pavilion. These kids called her "Mrs. V." and they were crazy about her.

CHAPTER 4

1920 · Francesco Guiseppe Viverito

FRANCESCO
GUISEPPE
VIVERITO
DRESSED AS A
GENTLEMAN
UNTIL
IT WAS TIME TO
CLEAN THE
CESSPOOL

The designers of the new Second Avenue subway stations has captured the 1940s in the tile artwork. It is almost like visiting a museum on Third Avenue and Sixty-third street. New York has five boroughs, and one in Brooklyn, where I lived growing up. The finished artwork: tile people on the wall could be my whole family. The mothers are dressed up, wearing woolen coats and high heels. The most meaningful to me looks like my father, whom I miss very much. He never left the house without wearing polished shoes, a suit with a vest, a white shirt and tie, and an overcoat when needed. Of course, his hat was the crowning glory. It was not unusual to see men dressed like this every day.

My father did not go to an office. He was a dental technician, and he worked in a lab he owned with a partner and where many perfect sets of false teeth were created. Uppers and Lowers looked different because of the palate across the uppers. Sometimes they looked like they could have a conversation.

My father had other clothes at the lab until I visited him when I was 12 and saw that the men wore khaki-colored pants and over-shirts with short sleeves.

"Daddy," as we never stopped calling him, was highly talented and could fix anything. He made a charm bracelet for our mother out of solid gold. Using plastic animals that were prizes in the cereal boxes, he made impressions of them filled with gold. There were probably 25 little animals swinging gaily from the gold bracelet.

He was easy to be with as he was soft-spoken, never raising his voice, and we only wanted to please him. He loved a bargain, and at one point in our lives, he got a great deal of grain alcohol from someone who owed him money. He would never let anything go to waste because he had known poverty. He began to make cordials out of the alcohol using a big pot on our kitchen stove—very interesting because he did not drink alcohol. I remember the cordials cooking, but I do not remember anyone drinking them.

One of the things I remember most was his hatred of the tele-phone company. When the bills arrived, he would dress in old clothes trying to look down and out and take the account down to the company office to see if they would reduce it. It is not known if it worked, but he never stopped trying. After we moved to Long Island and had his dental lab in the back of our house, he had a payphone installed, and we were supposed to make all our calls on it. However, we did not use change. He had taken three Bunsen burners and emptied them until they sounded like you were dropping in a coin. When you hit them with a knife, the sounds mimicked that of nickels, dimes, and quarters. Once he hit the burner too hard, and the operator said, "That sounded like a 50-cent piece," and my daddy said, "That would be silly; you can't get a 50-cent piece into the slot." Eventually, the telephone company took the payphone out of our house, saying that it was not used enough and there was not enough money.

We had a summer home in the country. There were no city sewers as there had been in Brooklyn. All the waste from showers and toilets went into what was known as a cesspool. It looked like a gigantic flowerpot before it was buried in the yard. This became another thing to fix, as he never knew he could hire somebody to suck out the cesspool. When he thought it was getting a little bit full, he would put a ladder down into it and climb down the ladder and empty it with buckets. I have no idea where he put the waste, but there was a forest behind our house, and I guess that's where it went. Even as an adult, when I saw him going down the ladder, the last thing to disappear would be his hat; I would be very nervous that he would fall in. He never did!

If he could do a job himself, he would never pay someone else. He poured concrete, made staircases, worked with wiring and electricity, fixed any plumbing problems in the country house, and always remained calm. However, he spoke Italian while doing it. We assume he was swearing.

If you gave him a compliment or a hug or just told him how much you loved him in so many ways, his shoulders would rise and shake slightly as if what you said gave him a chill. What my sisters and I wouldn't give to sit with him for a few hours.

He was a bit of a hypochondriac. When my husband was in medical school, he would have him perform tests. He bought a blood pressure cuff and would have his pressure taken and then run up the stairs in front of our house and repeat the test. He bought dipsticks to test his urine, and he would put a sample into a beer glass and have my husband check it. He would wash the glass and put it in his office cabinet to be used again.

 One of the worst times he chose to save money was my sister Janet's wedding. He ordered her cake from a friend who gave him a real deal, but the cake had to be picked up. My sister's friend, Claire, drove, and Janet sat in the back seat, holding the cake on her lap. Claire made a quick turn into our driveway, and the cake split. Janet came into the house holding her cake together and crying and screaming. My dad quietly spoke. Pointing to my husband, he said, "Eddie is a doctor. He can fix it." He ran to the store and came back with five cans of Reddi Whip. The cake was put back together with knitting needles, and Daddy stood over my husband as he repaired it with whipped cream.

Francesco is a man to be remembered!

CHAPTER 5

1943 · Ehelyn & Irma / Rachel & Robin: The Ladies of Third Street

 When rummaging through the 40 years of accumulation in our basement, we discovered a large round can holding old 16 mm family movies of us in Prospect Park. The last batch included our friends, the Gallaghers. My father took hundreds of home movies, often moving the camera too fast, causing a little motion sickness as you try to follow, but I am so grateful to have them today.

The movie tells the story of our mothers, who are friends and fashion mavens. Rachel and I are dressed in little coats, hats, and dresses. It might be Easter. My father is in a three-piece suit, a topcoat, and a hat. Men wore such formal clothing in the 1940s. Janet is asleep in an English pram with frilly white coverings. In the film, Rachel and I run to the slides while Ethelyn and Irma chat on a park bench. I think my mother loved hearing stories about Ethelyn's early romance with her boyfriend-boss, a wealthy man who took her dancing at The Rainbow Room. He showered her with gifts of jewelry from Tiffany's.

They wear straight coats, cloche hats, and gloves in the film. Their shoes look like something nuns wore, heavy and black. As Harry, Ethelyn's brother, said, "They were tight." Ethelyn would often spend time talking to Irma on the phone in the evening, and the two friends would smoke. My mother would continue sewing on the machine while her friend watched and spilled out her stories. She had some doubts about her boyfriend. My mother was older, so maybe she was giving her advice. At night Rachel did not come to our house. I was at her home more often, but without my mother. Ethelyn worked at a secretarial job and was gone during the day. We spent a great deal of time with Rachel's grandmother, who often gave us tastes of her Armenian dishes. I enjoyed my time there because I did not have a living grandmother.

Today, Rachel is a published author. Remembering our days on Third Street, she sent me the following:

#1. I remember ice skating one snowy Christmas morning at the Old Stone House playground on Third Street and Fifth Avenue. You had heard I got a new pair of ice skates, rang my bell, and said, "Let's go skating!"

#2. On rainy days, you would say, "Let's go skating in the Ninth Street subway station." There were long rolling passages we raced over, and we often glided on our skates down Third Street from the park.

#3. Every Friday, our mothers took us to the Chinese restaurant on Ninth Street. We ordered chop suey or chicken chow mein, egg rolls, spareribs, and wonton soup. It was greasy but delicious.

#4. You took me to your father's office, and you showed me a room with a table piled high with pairs of false teeth, and they were the "rejects." I asked about a pair of false buck teeth on the table, and you told me, "People want false teeth to look like their real teeth." That surprised me. Today people want perfect, white teeth.

#5. You would call out from your living room window to me in the street. We had lots of impromptu get-togethers at your house.

When my childhood friend, Mary Pat, phoned me from her home in Florida and said she had a message from Rachel Gallagher, I got pins and needles. After moving from Third Street, Rachel and I did not keep in touch, and Rachel found Mary Pat Meade through the Saint Saviour's High School registry. We don't skate anymore, but we go to lunch and Broadway and Off-Broadway. We shop! Our mothers would have liked that but would be appalled at the clothing of our time.

CHAPTER 6

1944 · Aunts & Uncles: The Lego Pieces of My Life

The Danish people had an excellent idea when they invented Legos. Anyone can use them to build whatever they see in their mind's eye. I imagine I am made of Legos, each piece influenced by someone important in my life.

Literature tells us that cousins are our first friends. This is true for me. I have many cousins from all over, and a few are exceptional. Cousins are aunts' and uncles' children, our parents' siblings. Our genetics and our Legos are from two large families: McAvoy's and Viveritos's. I can line my cousins up like a Lego army.

My mother, Rose Irma Theresa McAvoy, had one sister and four red-headed, freckle-faced brothers.

In my head, I list them in chronological order: Robert, Edward, Thomas, Eileen, Irma (my mother), and Kenny, the baby. They lived in Brooklyn in a comfortable home across Prospect Park. My grandfather owned a livery service. Sometimes, the children would be driven to school in one of the impressive cars. Arriving this way gave them an air of superiority, which they carried through life. I picture their garage with black, shiny Legos lined up in a row.

We don't know too much about their childhood, but they loved each other very much, so it was happy. The older two boys were wild and always in trouble; the third son, Tommy, was the best. Kenneth, the youngest, adored his two most senior brothers and imitated them to the detriment of his life later. I see them as three Legos lying on their sides, having been knocked over. These were the children of the McAvoy family, our aunts and uncles. They were an eclectic bunch. The two older brothers, Robert and Edward, died of tuberculosis, which was ravaging many young people. I never knew them. Still, my first Lego is Robert, for whom I am named.

Uncle Tommy was our favorite; his wife, Aunt Dorothy, was a country cook. Her pots were in color, like Legos. They lived on dairy farms and hired farmers to run them. In addition to living on the farm, they owned hardware and auto parts stores. They built them up, sold them at a nice profit, and then moved to another area with a need for that business. They repeated the process many times, and we loved seeing their new towns. They always had beautiful, old country houses in upstate New York. We visited them often and felt very comfortable with them. When my boyfriend (now husband) was at Cornell, we visited their nearby farm independently. I was crazy about them and wanted him to meet them. We meant to go just for the day, but we slept overnight. Aunt Dorothy had me sleep in a room with her and reminded me that she was a light sleeper.

Ducky and Tommy, their children, were older than us. When Ducky was little, she had yellow, blonde flyaway hair earning her nickname. It stuck. I remember Tommy and Patty at the top of a hill on their wedding day. Patty was lovely in her white dress, and Tommy was tall, thin, and impressive in his Army uniform. World War II had ended, and they were stationed in the US. We did not have to worry about them. This day was the Lego we held in our minds planning what kind of weddings we would like.

My mother's only sister, Aunt Eileen, graduated from the Fashion Institute of Technology in New York City. She and my mother made all their clothing and wore a very sophisticated high style. They copied the fashion of several movie stars, using Vogue patterns. Eileen was a scary one. We were not to call her Aunt as she said, in her gravelly voice, "Ants crawl on the ground!"

I often went to stay with them overnight in Scarsdale. Eileen was divorced and supported by the girls' father, Frank Carey, who owned a packaging company. My cousins often had Revlon samples for us to take home. I was close to her four daughters. Michelle joined the military and was quite successful. Nancy discovered the state teaching schools and talked her father, Frank Carey, into paying the tuition. She called Elise and said, "Get up here, the deals are fabulous, and Frank will pay our tuition. Stephanie, the youngest, was fun, but she suffered from clinical depression later in life. Elise married a man named Hank, who turned out to be gay. The marriage was never consummated and was annulled. We were not given the details, but Hank moved into our town 40 years later. He was running a big box store. My father loved to shop and discovered Hank working as the manager during a visit to Amsterdam. Of course, he asked Hank for a discount.

Eileen, my mother's sister, took a drug called Phenobarbital. She spoke with a British accent and could give you the scariest looks. She always wore black and walked as if she were floating. In a very husky voice, Eileen spat out orders. We learned to be quiet around adults. She was like Morticia from the Addams family, adding a bun and eyeglasses to her skinny appearance.

Uncle Kenny, the youngest, had five children. He was a sailor who was often at sea. Each time he came home, Aunt Ann got pregnant. They were very poor, living in a musty basement apartment. Aunt Ann worked outside the home to support them. When she visited us at the lake, I admired her bathing suit. She said she ordered it by mail, and my mother was surprised she would buy it from a catalog. There was nothing called online in 1950. "I know I may have to send something back," Aunt Ann told my mom, "But I don't mind making a package." I often think about that because, as her Lego, I shop online and keep packaging materials handy for returns. I often think of her while wrapping something to return. She would have loved Amazon.

Uncle Kenny came to see my mom when I was nine and home from school with a cold. Mom had gone to the rental library because the books she had ordered were ready. She was a great reader, and this Lego was passed down to us.

Ebinger's, a famous bakery, was next door to the Lending Library. I was sure she was getting their Blackout cake for us. Though our meals were delicious Irish stews and roasts, we rarely had dessert. Dinner always included potatoes and bread and butter. We ate things like tongue and kidneys and liver during the war years. Some of them tested like wooden Legos.

I offered Uncle Kenny coffee; he looked young and cute in his white sailor's uniform. At first, I didn't realize he was drunk until he asked me to look at the fish tank with him. "Watch this, all the little fishies are shitting, and the shits are sliding to the bottom." He was giggling." I called my father at work and whispered: "Uncle Kenny is here, he is drunk, and Mommy is not back yet." In 15 minutes, my father arrived and said kindly, "Kenny, you know better than to come here in this condition. Come with me. I will drive you home."

There were six children on the Viverito side in a townhouse on Seventh Avenue and Third Street. The three older sisters, Gertrude, Helen, and Anita, took care of their two baby brothers: my father and Uncle John.

Joseph and Gertrude were born in Sicily and traveled by ship to America with their parents. Anita, Helen, John, and my father, Frank, were born in Brooklyn. The family was not well off and lived in a rented brownstone on Third Street and Seventh Avenue in Brooklyn. Their father, our grandfather, had been a blacksmith in Sicily. A significant number of Legos gave us our love of horses. When my father, Frank (Francesco Guiseppe), was ten years old, my grandfather lost his leg in a railroad accident. With his knowledge of metals and iron, he was hired by the Pennsylvania Railroad. The company settled with him for a pitiful amount of money. They got away with it because he didn't speak English well and didn't know the law. After this accident, he became a tyrant, stomping around the house on a wooden peg leg and calling out, *"Silencio!"* All the children were afraid of him. If they tried to talk to him, he would say *"Stat a zeet,"* which means "shut up," and "Fotch a dausta," translated to a fresh face.

In high school, I broke my ankle and had a walking cast. One evening, my father told me that he got scared whenever he heard me coming. That was when we heard stories of our grandfather. He was unkind to my grandmother, Josephine, who her children adored. My cousin, Patti, told me he hit Josephine when angry. I am sure that when his boys got bigger, this stopped. Francesco Viverito returned to Sicily to live out the rest of his life, leaving his family with little means of support. Not much is known after that, but he is buried in a village near Alta Villa. The photo of his gravestone speaks volumes. The largest statue in the cemetery in the shape of a cross leads one to believe that this was a prominent, wealthy man. The megalomaniac had spent the remaining Railroad settlement money on his headstone. Meanwhile, his wife was taking in washing and ironing in Brooklyn to feed their children.

I found a census taken in 1910. It notes that the census of 1890 was destroyed by fire. It also states that this might be used as a birth certificate. It lists my aunts and uncles by their Italian names, which

I never knew: Joseph, the oldest, was 15 in 1910. It shows that they left Italy in 1899 and that my grandfather Crescenzo had taken out naturalization papers in 1899.

Josephine Damiano was my grandmother, and she was adored by her children. All of them had Italian names, which became anglicized when they arrived. Aunt Gertrude's name was Geardy, Helen was called Nellie, and Aunt Anita had the nickname Annie. Uncle John's Italian name was Giovanni and Frank was Francesco.

Left to right: Aunt May, Uncle John, Mom, Dad, & Aunt Anita

The Viverito children learned to take care of each other. They worshipped their mother, Josephine, who died about two months after I was born, so although she knew me, I never knew her. She instilled deep love and respect. Her children supported each other and adored all their nieces and nephews. Still, their loyalty to each other transcended it all.

At one time, my husband and I brought our 12-year-old daughter and her horse to a horse show on Long Island so that our families could see her compete. Stony Brook is about five hours from our home in upstate New York, longer if you pull a horse trailer. I so wanted my father to see her ride. He lived only 15 miles from Stony

Brook. He did not come to the show, which lasted three days. After having a leg amputated, Aunt Gertrude was in the hospital, and he and his sisters went every day to sit by her bed and pray. I was dreadfully disappointed. My cousin Patti gave me a copy of the book *Blood of My Blood* to help me understand. The book is about the southern Italians, and this Viverito family is almost religious proof of the theory. They were raised to believe that the six were the most influential people in the world to each other, before wives and children. They were like a block of intertwined Legos that could not be broken.

Somehow, they managed to get degrees. Joseph, whom they always referred to with reverence as "Our Brother Joe", became the patriarch and called the shots until his death at age 84. He became a dentist and took care of all his nieces and nephews, who simultaneously loved and feared him. He would stuff our mouths with cotton and say, "No Novocain for you, you are a free patient."

Uncle Joe and Aunt Marie lost a daughter my age. Jean, a cousin we all loved dearly. They gave us a lovely engagement party at their beautiful home in Garden City. I think they wanted me to have whatever they could have given Jean.

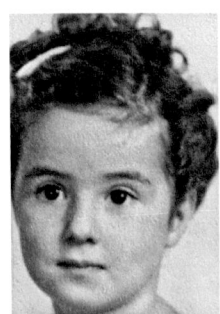 

Aunt Marie reminded Uncle Joe that he had to get the flowers the night before. Uncle Joe turned to my fiancé and said, "Eddie, you come and help me." Eddie wondered what florist would be open now, but a florist was not the destination. He handed Eddie a considerable container to carry, and they went for a walk along Fifth Street, where they lived. Hydrangea bushes were in full bloom, and when Uncle Joe began to cut them and throw them to Eddie, he realized that there was no florist. The flowers were so abundant that no one would notice. When a car came down the street with its lights on, Uncle Joe jumped out of sight, and Eddie followed him. The flower arrangements were gorgeous. Aunt Helen and Uncle Joe Caravella provided us with two lovely cousins, Patti and Terry. Aunt Helen took us to the Meadow at Prospect Park. She packed a lunch of tiny lettuce and tomato sandwiches on Parker House rolls, cookies, grapes, and lemonade. Aunt Helen taught us how to roll down a hill in our little dresses, making sure we kept our knees together and our arms folded over our chests like straight Legos. When I stopped to visit her soon after I became engaged, she had a white peignoir set for me as a gift. She showed her love for us by celebrating things like that. I resemble her more than either of her daughters. Uncle Joe Caravella was always giving us advice. When we were teenagers, he told us, "It is as easy to marry a rich man as it is to marry a poor one." This was interesting as he also said, "My underwear was made from flour sacks when I was a kid."

We are all proud of Uncle Joe's five years overseas during World War II, taking care of the young wounded American soldiers. Many years later, my own husband, Eddie, would do the same thing in Vietnam.

Aunt Anita, whose fiancé had been killed in WWII, never married. She was very skinny and reminded us of Olive Oyl, Popeye's girlfriend. Aunt Anita brought us tins of butter cookies from A&S, where she worked. She told us we must always have office skills, so we studied typing in high school and insisted we wash the dishes under hot, running water. She was the maiden aunt, always there for her siblings in a crisis. When my Lego hands are rinsing dishes, I often think of Aunt Anita. She moved in and helped her sister Helen care for her family and live with the fear that her young husband might never come home from the war.

Aunt Gertrude was a seamstress who taught sewing at Julia Richmond High School. She held a master's degree in Fashion Design from NYU. Her husband, Uncle Tony, never worked, always dressed to the nines. Uncle Tony spent most of his day in the Blue Eagle, a gentlemen's bar on the corner of Third Street. When we were on our way home from school, he would jump out to scare us. He belonged to the St. George club in Brooklyn, and occasionally, he would take us all there to swim. He had one of those skimpy swimsuits that were popular in Europe. I was always glad when he got into the water, so I didn't have to look at him. The Legos were showing.

They had no children, by choice, as he was the child. He was fun and caused no trouble within the family. At his funeral, Aunt Gertrude asked that we all call out "Goodbye, Tony" as the coffin was lowered. Of course, we all did just that.

Uncle John and Aunt Mae had five children, and every summer, the oldest, Johnny, came to live with us at the lake. He was and still is the brother we didn't have. Johnny was a groomsman at our wedding. The bridal party went to the beach in the afternoon before the rehearsal dinner, and Johnny, who had a small bridge for two teeth, lost it in the ocean. Daddy told him to keep his mouth hydrated. The priest gave him a lecture at the rehearsal because he was chewing gum in church. I jumped to his defense. Blood of my blood will not be accosted, even by a priest. My father, a dental technician, stayed up late, making Johnny a new bridge for the morning's wedding. His Lego look is teeth on a wire.

Uncle John was a physical education teacher at Brooklyn Tech and was a great swimmer. His wife, Aunt Mae, was the person from whom we learned the importance of Italian cooking. I am not much of a cook. That Lego piece slipped away, but I like to have every relative and friend around my table. On holidays she often served us orange soda with a bit of red wine. The Sicilians had many citrus trees in their small towns, and they mixed the fruit with wine, hence the orange drink. This may be why I love Sangria served with colored straws resembling Legos. She was very loving and showed it with cooking. Aunt Mae was also a fashion plate when she was young. Later, she would have a beautiful dress at family weddings, and when mealtime came, she would put on a gold lame bib. When Johnny came to visit us in upstate New York, he would bring trays of eggplant parmesan, bowls of sauce, and meatballs to be frozen so I could serve them later. Aunt May's Lego is the handle of a pot.

When our son Christopher got married, I used silk flower arrangements. Aunt Mae asked me if she could take one home, and I said, "Of course." Her eyes filled with tears, and she said, "I want to put them on Daddy's grave," meaning Uncle John.

My cousins all loved my father, Frank, as he was fun and almost always smiling. He could fix anything from a broken chair to a turkey that was too big for the oven. One Thanksgiving, he took the enormous turkey, covered it with a brown bag, and stepped on it until it fit. His Lego was a screwdriver with some teeth on the handle.

It is said that you can choose your friends, but not your family. However, if I had the choice, I would have kept that cast of characters, all of whom had some influence on my life. I have Lego pieces from each of them that hold my childhood memories.

CHAPTER 7

1945 · Our Areaway in Park Slope: 474 Third Street

Brooklyn has suffered the brunt of jokes throughout the years. Listen to a five-minute excerpt from Milton Berle, Ed Sullivan, Jerry Lewis, or Brooklyn and Bronxie. I lived in Brooklyn for a good portion of my life and never heard of "toity toid street."

Brooklyn was a small town in the 1940s, with each neighborhood defined by the church parish and the schools. Third Street, where we lived, had some brownstones with steps to the second floor, limestones, and apartment houses not more than six stories high. In front of each apartment house was a broad "stoop" of three or four steps framed by side walls with lions or other animal heads carved on pillars at each side. The mothers sat here while their children played in their own space surrounded by a decorative black wrought iron fence with a swinging gate. I have not found a definition for this

150-foot rectangle of concrete called an areaway, pronounced airy way. Stoop is an essential word in the language of this city.

No one dared to venture into an areaway without an invitation, and heaven help the guest from another building who caused trouble. The 12 or so children who lived in that building immediately became a family and would gang up on this outsider screaming, "Get out of our areaway!" The shamed culprit would slink home quietly.

Maple trees line Third Street right up to the park where there had been a stately entrance to the Litchfield Mansion. Third Street is wider than other Park Slope streets. Some people think it was the approach for horses and carriages.

In the mid-1940s, few people had cars in Brooklyn, so there was very little traffic, making the street an extension of the play area. The oncoming ice cream truck bells prompted us to call our moms for money. We would line up at the white truck, and the ice-cream man, dressed in a crisp white uniform and cap, would serve us. I always got a Charlotte Russe, a small cake with whipped cream swirled four inches high.

We would return to our areaway with our treats, and Third Street would be tranquil for a while. These ice cream days were special for us as we rarely had dessert at home. My mother was an excellent cook; we had stews, roasts, and mashed potatoes, always with bread and butter and ice-cold milk. We kept milk in the icebox next to the massive block of ice. Eugenio, the iceman, came every few days, driving his horse and wagon. He was grumpy, and we never bothered him. He had giant tongs with which he lifted the block of ice and would carry it to our kitchen. Some visiting merchants sharpened knives and scissors; another wagon led by a large brown horse arrived with farm vegetables arranged colorfully with green cabbages, red tomatoes, oranges, peppers, and bright yellow bananas. Moms up and down the street would appear with their wallets and brown bags.

The ubiquitous man with a camera would photograph you sitting on his pony. He hid his head under a black hood to snap your picture. The parents paid, and the photos arrived in a week. I wonder now who was holding that pony. Knowing horses as I do now, I guess the poor animal was drugged.

The areaway had stairs and a door to the cellar, but only the landlord went down there. It was so dark and scary. We would put our garbage on the dumbwaiter, which opened near the kitchen, with ropes to move it up or down and send it to the cellar for him to remove. He was spooky, but his wife, Mrs. Lobiletto, was nice to us. Our youngest sister, Muffin, was always in trouble with him for making noise or jumping in the hallway. She played with his daughter, Ariella, and she even caused Ariella to lose a tooth one day.

We moved out of that house in 1954, when Muffin was nine years old. In 1984 we took a nostalgic tour of Brooklyn with our cousins when Terry came to visit from Portland, Oregon. Aunt Anita decided to join us. Johnny drove his station wagon to 474 Third Street, parked outside, and crossed the Areaway. We checked our old apartment's mailbox and discovered that Mrs. Lobiletto lived there. We knocked on the door, and Mrs. Lobiletto answered. I said, "Our father was Frank Viverito. We used to live here." She looked us over for a moment, then tears filled her eyes, and she embraced my youngest sister crying, "Maffy, Maffy."

When I remember Brooklyn, it is always with joy. We lived through the blackouts of World War II and, later, fear of the Russians. We had air raids and airplane searchlights and learned to hide under our desks in school during air raid drills wearing dog tags around our necks to identify us. Our father went out as a warden wearing a hard hat, running the lamp that searched the skies for enemy planes. We ate kidney stew and tongue and Spam. We squeezed a plastic bag with a red dot in the middle until it turned yellow and became a substitute for butter.

In those days, I woke up each morning ready for a new adventure. I organized small parades up and down Third Street, singing. A favorite song was 'Over There'. We shouted,

"The Yanks are coming, and We won't come back until it's over… over there."

CHAPTER 8

1946 · In the Little Red Schoolhouse

In 1905 Father Flood purchased an English Mansion on Eighth Avenue and Seventh Street for $18,000. The main building on Sixth Street was crowded. First to fourth grade had been moved to a brick schoolhouse. New classrooms had been added and the upstairs remodeled as a home for the School Sisters of Notre Dame.

There was a lovely entrance into a center hall, and the first classroom was Sister Andre's. She was waiting for us at the double doors which framed her desk in the front of the room.

This desk is an example of the desks used in the 1900s. These were bolted to the floor at all four legs, two across and six down, putting 12 immovable desks in a double row.

There was a small cubby for supplies and books, an inkwell that I remember using, and a slot for a pencil. When you were called to answer a question, you stood by the side of the chair, which flipped up.

One side of the room was all windows. The school did not usually close for summer until the end of June. It could be hot during spring and early summer.

The blackboard ran the length of the other long wall. I shared my desk place with Kevin McLoughlin, who was from an extensive and prominent family. Members of this family would show up from time to time throughout my life. I liked sitting with Kevin even though he was a boy. He had lots of sandy hair, and it was always shiny, and he smelled clean. When Sister asked me to give out papers, and I could get out of my seat and parade around the room, I felt very important.

One day as I came back to my seat, Kevin had his hand over my name, covering a Silver Star and 100 percent on my math paper. He was so nice for a boy. We are still friends.

Sometimes, as Sister Andre walked near our desks to check our work, she would put her hand down on my desk. Her hand was tiny and so clean, even under the nails. In the future, I would wash my hands as often as I could to keep the scent lingering.

Students at Saint Saviour's wore uniforms: the girls wore a white short-sleeved blouse with a Peter Pan collar under a navy-blue jumper with a pleated skirt. White socks and sturdy shoes were required. The boys wore navy pants, white shirts, and ties. Kevin had this short little tie made of a strong, woven fabric.

When we arrived at school in the morning, we would hang our clothing in the cloakroom. Some days, we wore galoshes (boots that go over shoes and clip in a line down the front).

We stood by the sides of our desks to recite the Hail Mary and the Pledge of Allegiance. When we were called to answer questions, we stood in the same manner as a sign of respect.

We went home for lunch most days. The nuns called it dinner and had lunch in the convent. As students went home for lunch, we must have had an hour. Mom always had a hot lunch made with last night's dinner leftovers. A typical lunch might be creamed cauliflower on toast.

On rainy days we brought our lunch in black metal pails. The lunchroom was in the basement near the lavatories, and it smelled like peanut butter, jelly, and urine.

Our first-grade classroom was in a satellite building, a little red brick building with six classrooms, all on the first floor. Our classroom on the right side opened with double doors, and we were immediately in the front of the room. We passed Sister's desk on the right as we headed for the cloakroom in the back of the room.

The blackboard covered the right-side wall where Kevin and I sat, and it was clean in the morning but covered with chalk dust by 3:00 p.m. It was an exceptional honor to be asked to go outside and clap the erasers. We were too small to reach the top of the blackboard, so I imagine Sister Andre washed the board. When I became a teacher, washing the blackboard was my least favorite task. The chalk does not come off quickly, and you must keep rinsing the sponge for each swipe: top to bottom, in straight lines always. Next, you got the wastebasket and cleared off all the chalk dust, sliding it toward the end of the grooved wooden ledge that held the chalk and right into the basket.

The large school's front entrance on Sixth Street is a massive staircase wide enough to hold many children. I think the stairs were slate, and on the side of the railing, steel curlicues traveled up to four stories and had many turns. Halfway up between the first and second floor was the entrance to the convent. It had a steel door looking like a bank vault with locks on both sides. No child ever walked through these doors, not even when we were in high school. This foreboding door was the nuns' entrance to the convent, and I assume it came out on the second or third floor on the other side.

After school, we changed our clothes and went out to play in the section of our apartment house, which was called the areaway. We did lots of jumping rope and roller skating. Jump rope could include everyone so often we decided to play that. There were two "turners" to begin with, and they would have a rope about twelve feet to allow space for jumping in or out.

One popular rhyme was
"All in together, girls,
How do you like the weather, girls?"
the next girl picks it up, jumps in, and speaks
"January, February." Another girl can jump in and try to pick up at the month just reached. My favorite jump rope game was the alphabet, just as it says below.
A My name is Alice,
I come from Alabama.
My sister's name is Ann,
We live on The Avenue
I love to eat an apple.

I could do this to the end of the alphabet, but I could not jump for that long.

You were allowed to make up your own story: I loved this one:

R MY NAME IS ROBIN.

I was called Roberta in school but not at home. When we moved many years later, I registered as Robin. When I sent this story to Kevin, he said, "You will always be Roberta to me."

CHAPTER 9

1948 · Anatomy of a Day in Brooklyn

Waking up in my small but very own bedroom, I would carefully make my bed and shove anything else in the room under it. I arrange my dolls and stuffed animals on the top of the bed and carefully put away the chemistry set I used last night to make invisible ink. My blue jumper with the pleated skirt goes on over my white Peter Pan-collared blouse. Our apartment is known as a railroad flat. All the rooms come off one long hallway, so I turn right towards the apartment's front. There is one more oversized bedroom behind me. I pass the bathroom, long and skinny with small tiles in black and white checks, the style of the 1940s. I walk quickly past the dumbwaiter, just in case a mouse lurks inside the door. It is where we put our trash at night. It looks like a small door. When you open it, you pull on the roes to bring it to your floor kitchen.

I make toast or cheerios and pour a glass of milk. The kitchen is large by city standards. The interesting art of this kitchen is a huge rack that descends from the ceiling on a pulley. Mom hung the wet clothing on this rack, and we pulled it to the top and hooked it. These indoor clotheslines were used when the weather was too bad to dry outside. Brooklyn has a mild climate, and it rarely snows.

At 8:30 a.m., I leave the apartment through the entrance hall, where my grandmother's cedar chest holds a lamp and an empty crystal vase. The coat closet is there, and the front door. I step outside the linoleum-covered landing, large enough to stage a play. There are six floors, with two apartments on each, and we hold plays and dance lessons on different levels.

 Jumping down one flight of stairs and past the 12 locked mailboxes, I cross the stoop with small concrete lions on either side. Dropping off the stoop, I land in the areaway, a gated front yard made of concrete, surrounded by a black wrought iron fence. Now, I have an empty feeling in the pit of my stomach. Turning right, I head up Third Street to Seventh Avenue, cross the trolley tracks, and head for Mary Cook's house. I always call for someone on my way to school, and I planned with girls the day before. Park Slope is famous for its 19th-century architecture and beautiful homes, many probably listed as historic preservation buildings.

Seventh Avenue is commercial, and it divides the neighborhood with trolley tracks. My friends who seem to have fathers who have essential jobs live up the street in one-family homes. Our friends Dr. and Mrs. Barone lived in a lovely townhouse with a small yard. We often had dinners there on Sunday, and Mrs. Barone would use china and crystal. Many years later, traveling in Italy, I would find the same baroque, hand-painted Murano glass and buy it. I also bought a teapot and cups, which I cannot use. The spout on the teapot is too close to the bottom. The water runs out through the spout when you try to fill it. The handle on the teacups is too low and unbalanced to hold. Nevertheless, it looks marvelous in the china closet and makes a good story.

Third Street above Seventh Avenue has everything from tiny, dark apartments to magnificent brownstones and limestone homes. My friend, Mary, lives in a three-story limestone with a curved front. The large living room is white and graciously decorated with over-stuffed white couches and chairs. It opens into a large dining room with polished wooden furniture and another fireplace. The kitchen is in the back, unseen. Upstairs, the bedrooms all have carved fire-places. Almost all the bedrooms have twin beds, dressing tables, and comfortable chairs. They often share a bathroom with another identical bedroom. Many windows with beautiful draperies open for the sunlight to be allowed in. A four-foot nook is in the wall as the staircase rounds halfway to the second floor. Mary's mom had placed a three-foot-tall statue of the Blessed Virgin in that spot. I recently learned that many of the brownstones have the same alcoves. Did everyone need a Blessed Virgin or the Infant of Prague in there? This architecture was indented at the turns, so coffins could be turned, removing the dead from home. There was a custom to hold a wake at home instead of a funeral home. Mary's father has number one on his license plate, and I don't know why, and I think it is important. My father's license plate is 5K54, but the number is essential only to our family.

We all leave together following our morning session and retrace our steps along Eighth Avenue to Sixth Street. Sometimes we cross Eighth and walk down past Methodist Hospital, where my uncle, my godfather, has his practice. In an hour, we must be back, so we all walk home quickly. I look forward to lunch because it is always something warm and leftover from last night's dinner. Today it is creamed cauliflower on toast, and my younger sisters are waiting for me. Soon, they will go to school, and I won't call for anyone. After eating my lunch, brushing my teeth, and combing my hair again, I get Mary, and we line up in front of the school where the nuns are waiting. Each class is assigned a spot. Sometimes, when a nun turns sideways in the sunlight, I can see her hair under her veil. It always fascinates me that they keep their hair. I thought they all shaved their heads and had hysterectomies. I never asked anyone.

Everyone has arrived in just a few minutes, and she takes out her clicker. We are trained to become silent at the sound and follow her respectfully into the school and up the stairs. Three o'clock and we are free. We hang around the corners many days with the boys and girls we know well. Eventually, we leave, saying, "See you tomorrow," answered by, "Not if I see you first."

On my way home, I would pass the Blue Eagle, a bar on the corner of Third Street and Seventh Avenue. Here is another uncle who did not work at Methodist Hospital or anywhere. I try to avoid Uncle Tony, married to my father's sister. Aunt Gertrude is a teacher at Julia Richmond High School in Manhattan. While she is teaching, Uncle Tony keeps house. Then he carefully dresses for the day, ensuring his beautiful clothes and shoes are as neat and shiny as his bald head. If he sees me, he will run out to greet me and then try to drag me into the Blue Eagle to introduce me to everyone. "I'm late today, Uncle Tony, and I have a lot of homework." Soon, I am back in my area with my sisters and other kids in the neighborhood. We will play until 5:00 p.m., sometimes in the street, playing ringalevio or kick the can. We jump rope to the alphabet, "A, my name is Anna," begins the game. The following person jumps in and calls, "I live in Alabama." My friend, Rachel, lives across the street in a four-story brownstone. Rachel and her family live on the first two floors. They rent out the upper floors, and an impressive outdoor staircase leads to the apartments. We sometimes play "school" on these steps.

I am always the teacher, and if the student answers a question correctly, they may move up a step. Sometimes we sit in her beautiful living room in front of the fireplace and make random phone calls. Giggling so hard we can barely talk, we ask the unsuspecting person, "Is your refrigerator running?" We screech out when they say yes, "Go catch it." Later we will come up with better things like asking a woman if her husband is home and saying, "Well, I think I left my compact in his jacket pocket last night," all with our ten-year-old voices. This super fun game will only last six months; Rachel's grandmother catches us and makes us go outside to play with the other kids.

At 5:30 p.m. our moms open the windows and call us in for dinner. There are blackout shades to be pulled down at night, and Daddy goes somewhere in the neighborhood where he takes turns watching the sky with giant searchlights. It scares me when he goes, and I am always happy when it is not his turn. Then time for bed, and it begins all over again.

CHAPTER 10

1948 · Summers at The Lake

My mother was a voracious reader, and I don't remember her leaving the house very often. We came home for lunch, and she always had a hot lunch for us, leftovers from the night before. She was an excellent cook and prepared roasts, potatoes, stews, and gravies. We did not have desserts very often, although she could make a layer cake from scratch that none of us could reproduce.

She did not do a weekly shopping. All our food was purchased in small quantities and from neighborhood stores. Sometimes, she would send me to the store for "an eye of round" or to the lending library for some books she had on hold.

She had a wringer washing machine in the kitchen and an "ice box." We were all fascinated with the wringer machine, which had both a hose and the wringer over the sink. Above the stove was a metal gadget about five feet by seven feet. It had crossbars and clothespins ready. The laundry went from the wringer onto the dryer, which was raised to the ceiling by a pulley. She must have done the laundry in the evening because we ate dinner in that kitchen. I don't remember laundry hanging there during meals. There was also a clothesline strung across the yard from the window in the back bedroom and attached to another building. It was on pulleys, and in good weather, laundry was hung there. Next to the clothesline was a fire escape where pillows and blankets could be aired. The iceman came every few days with a massive chunk of ice that he lifted with black iron tongs.

Park Slope was considered a lovely place to live at that time. It went downhill after we moved, but Brooklyn was discovered by the "Yuppies" in the 1960s and really became desirable by 1990. Yuppies are young, upwardly mobile professionals. They made a good deal of money and liked to show off their success.

The identical apartments are called condos now, and the residents probably have refrigerators and send their laundry out. The cellars were dark and scary. We sent our garbage down on a dumb waiter, where we occasionally were greeted by a mouse as we opened the door.

My mother was fun! There were always visitors at our house. Mom had grown-up nieces, and they used to hang out with her. They were the children of her rather morbid sister and were happier at our home.

She had a few friends. My uncle was our doctor, and when he delivered a baby to an eighteen-year-old unmarried woman, who lived across the street, he asked Mom to befriend her. She was glamorous and often visited in the evening, sitting next to my mother at her sewing machine, both smoking and swapping stories.

My parents were happy when we were small. They had a victrola, and sometimes they would dance together in the living room as a treat for us. They did not go out very often. Mom went to her "meetings" religiously. Whether she drank during those years, I do not know. My uncle prescribed phenobarbital, a tranquilizer. Once in a while, Mommy would ask one of us to get her a "pheno." She did not get up with us for school, and we had chocolate pudding for breakfast. I knew how to make it, and we would eat it warm with broken graham crackers added to it. Perhaps the drug knocked her out. My friend, Mary Pat, spent a good deal of time at our house. She called me after she had seen the movie *"Divine Secrets of the YaYa Sisterhood."* Ashley Judd, also a redhead, reminded me of how much fun my mother had been during our summers at the lake. I asked her if she thought my mother drank then, as Ashley Judd had in the movie. Mary Pat was quiet for a moment, and then she said, "Maybe."

We often went to relatives for holidays, but sometimes, my mother would open an antique table in the living room. It probably seated about twelve. We would have apple cider in beautiful wine glasses. Once when we had company, I remember sauterne being served, but I can't remember if Mommy drank any.

We spent our summers in a small house in Lake Panamoka, about two hours out on Long Island. My dad came out for the weekends and on Wednesday nights, as did most of the fathers. Here, Mommy seemed to have more friends and was outside all the time. We went to the beach every day at the corner of our street. As we became teenagers, she started a teenage dance at the Pavilion, an open-air building for the residents' use. She would gather everything, the microphone, records, and kids. They all loved her and would often come to our cottage to visit her. She could do anything she wanted to, and I think "wanted" was the keyword.

She had a friend named "Aunt Lettie" who had two sons, and often the mothers would take us out in a rowboat on the lake at night. They had us singing, *"Show me the way to go home, I'm tired, and I want to go to bed. I had a little drink about an hour ago, and it went right to my head. No matter where I roam, over land or sea or foam, you will always find me singin' this song. Show me the way to go home."*

We loved these nights in the rowboat, and we all swam like fish.

This was the house we moved to from Brooklyn, and it was the beginning of the end. I will always wonder if I could have helped her if I had known then what I know now.

CHAPTER 11

1949 · If a Girl Whistles, The Blessed Mother Cries

I was six years old, leggy, and skinny when Pee Wee Reese gave me a nickel and said, "Call me in ten years." Only in Brooklyn would people be properly impressed by this encounter with a Brooklyn Dodger! In 1955, the city held a Welcome Back to Brooklyn Day.

Thousands of people from all over the US with perfectly adequate speech patterns returned to honor the city they love. Growing up in Brooklyn, New York, in the 1940s and 1950s was probably the best life a kid could have. Relatives all lived nearby, and children walked to school along the very wide, tree-lined streets and avenues of Park Slope. Early in the morning, the street cleaning machines with scrub brushes six feet in diameter, water shooting out through them, would have already been at work.

Marys, Johnnys, Rachels, and Maureens roller-skated in those streets and played kickball and ring-a-levio like all the other children in Brooklyn. Safety was taken for granted. On hot summer days, my father would emerge from our building with a big wrench and open the fire hydrant. Like magic, children ran up and down the block in bathing suits and beach shoes. Steam rose from the warm tar street, and soon, the ice-cream truck appeared almost as if he knew we would be there.

Four Seventy-four Third Street, pictured on the cover, was an apartment building made of white limestone, with lovely architecture and a very wide stoop, where we often gathered. Inside the building, each floor had two apartments and a linoleum-covered landing large enough for seven or eight kids to play.

Sometimes we would meet in the hallways. Donna lived on the top floor. Her mother, Vicki, would line us up outside her apartment and teach us to tap dance. "When I was younger," she would say, "I was a Rockette, and this is what we did. Now follow me, shuffle, shuffle, step, step." We rarely entered her immaculate apartment, but peeking in, you could see everything in its place.

In front of every apartment building, a wrought iron fence surrounded a concrete rectangle of approximately 50 x 100 feet, known as an areaway.

Children played within the confines of their own environment, mainly with the other children in the building. "Get out of our areaway," we would shout if someone who didn't live in our building tried to join us without an invitation.

Italian families with a million cousins got together on Sunday afternoon for a huge six-course meals! An orange crush with a bit of red wine was a special dinner treat.

 At Saint Saviour's School, nuns taught us as they had taught our father when he went there as a small boy. Sister Acquilla's Infant of Prague stood by the windows in her third-grade classroom, its several sets of clothing carefully stored underneath. If you were excellent that week, you could help change the Infant's outfit on Friday after school. I was chosen often. Not because of my behavior but because Sister Acquilla loved my father when he was a little boy. Sister's hands always smelled of soap as they protruded from the large sleeve of her floor-length sweeping black habit. Beneath this sleeve was a tight stockinet sleeve where she tucked her hanky. We often wondered how the black batiste veils were attached to the white, starched linen wimples. The veils were elbow length, and the Sisters' faces were encircled with white buckram, starched to the consistency of cardboard.

At eighteen in college, we were taught by the same School Sisters of Notre Dame. Sister Coralie, our house mother, showed us how they glued the head and face pieces together with Elmer's glue. At 60, I returned to Notre Dame, and the nuns were wearing street clothes. The effect was utterly disappointing. In their habits, these women were something to behold. Seeing Sister Coralie without hers, I felt I had lost something special.

My father, who loved Brooklyn, had not had an easy childhood. His parents and three older siblings scrunched together in third class on a ship that brought them to the United States from Sicily. They arrived with the three children and produced four more in Brooklyn. Daddy was the youngest and his three older sisters told him what to do until the day he died. He always obeyed them!

My grandfather was a blacksmith in the old country. His skill with iron earned him a spot as a railroad yard worker. He lost his leg when the brakes failed, pinning him between two cars. He never recovered from his resulting depression. Anger became a part of his personality, and he stomped menacingly about the house on his wooden leg. I never knew this until I broke my leg in high school and had a walking cast. My father often said that he thought his father was coming when he heard me walking. It scared him.

Grandfather returned to Sicily, leaving his family to fend for themselves. A determined and formidable woman with no education and not much English, my grandmother took in washing and ironing to keep her family together. By then, the older siblings were able to work. They lived at home and put their salaries in for maintenance and to help send some money to their oldest brother, Joe, who was in dental school at Penn.

It is incredible to think that this could happen despite their circumstances. From then on, the siblings were extremely proud of their oldest brother, DOCTOR Joseph Viverito. Until his retirement at 80, he was our personal dentist; he used to stuff our mouths with cotton and say, "You are free patients, no Novocain for you," then proceed to drill. To this day, my cousin Pattie dreads going to the dentist.

Every Sunday morning, we sang lovely Latin hymns at the children's mass in the church's basement. Supposedly the parents would go to mass in the church proper. Our parents dropped us off, and I don't think they went to church because they were already in the car waiting for us when we came out.

Our school uniform consisted of blue jumpers with white blouses and sturdy leather shoes. It was years before I realized that the nuns outlawed patent leather shoes because they thought the boys could see up our skirts in the shine of the patent leather.

 "If a girl whistles, the Blessed Mother cries," said Sister Acquilla. I believed her and have never, never learned to whistle. It probably made more of an impression on me than if she had said it was not ladylike to whistle.

Everyone knew everyone in the neighborhood where we lived. One evening the phone rang and it was the mechanic from the garage around the corner. "Frank," he said, "The Brooklyn Dodgers are in here with car trouble. Bring your girls over right away." That was the day I met Pee Wee Reese, Gil Hodges, and Carl Furillo.

Sometimes my father shot *craps* in front of the barbershop, a game played with dice for money. I often saw them on the way home from school when the odor of witch hazel wafted from the door next to the red and white revolving barber's pole. They were saying things like "Baby needs a new pair of shoes," as they threw the dice against the street wall.

Gambling was illegal. One day my mother called the police, tipped them off, dialed the shop, and said, "Frank, get out!" Daddy, who always a very soft-spoken soul, yelled loudly that night. The barber and his friends never blamed Daddy. They chalked it up to the fact that my Irish mother did not understand loyalty.

CHAPTER 12

1950 · The Loves of My Life

Lake Panamoka is a two-hour drive from Brooklyn, and somehow my parents found it and decided to spend a summer there. We rented a house on the lake with a screened porch, where my sisters and I played on rainy days. We had a batch of plastic baby dolls and a spaghetti pot with diving boards made of tongue depressors. The bare little kewpie doll babies supplied hours of fun on our screened porch on many rainy days.

The house came with a rowboat, so we were often taken out on the lake, where we picked water lilies and created lovely bowls of flowers. We built our own house the following summer and spent many winter weekends and entire summers there.

"Beep, beep, it's Wednesday," Mom would call on Wednesday mornings. "Beep, beep, it's Friday," was the morning cry. We did not have a car, and my mom, who grew up in the city, did not drive. Beep, beep meant that Daddy was driving out that night.

Renting a house in Lake Panamoka near Brookhaven National Laboratories was a far cry from renting a small mansion in the Hamptons., which they called cottages.

The Manhattanites flew past, driving two more hours to their COTTAGES on the east end of Long Island. Cottage, to us, meant cottage.

The neighbors were middle-class people who lived and worked in Brooklyn, Queens, and Nassau counties. Most were two or three small bedrooms, no dining rooms, screened-in porches, and small living rooms.

During the week, the population included moms and kids. There were three beaches, and we lived near the second beach. The lake, which swimmers had not used, had a muddy bottom. We put up with it until the Lake Panamoka Association dropped tons of clean sand on top of the muck, and with all the people swimming, it cleared up beautifully. As I grew older, I found that the cool kids hung out at the first beach and ventured to find friends. We formed a group of about 15 teenagers at the First Beach. At 13 and 14, this was an idyllic haven. We all put our blankets or towels together. We brought our lunch and ate it by the lagoon at the waterfront's edge.

One night, we discovered this was an excellent place to meet, build a fire, hang out, talk, or tell stories. It was an innocent time.

"Let's plan to walk to the Dairy Bar," Janice suggested, followed by a chorus of "Yes, yes!" The plan was made for the next day to go in the morning before it got too hot. The Dairy Bar, an ice-cream parlor in Wading River, was along a dirt road two miles away. The Nassau County Boy Scout Association owned the land on both sides.

There was a Boy Scout camp, which was not open to the public. In front of the entrance was a sign hanging from a tree.

"I think that I shall never see
A poem as lovely as a tree."
by Joyce Kilmer

We sang, we walked, we talked, and the boys teased all the girls. I had not had a boyfriend among this group or anywhere. I was in seventh grade, and although I didn't know it then, I was cute with a slim teenage figure. At one point, I found myself next to Ronnie Pederson, a tall blonde, blue-eyed 14-year-old. "I think Joan likes you," I told him. "Maybe you should walk faster and catch up with her." "Why should I catch up with Joan when I would rather be with you?" Ronnie questioned me, and I was stunned. "With me, why?" "Because it is you I like." Wow, I didn't know what to say, but Ronnie became my first boyfriend. He lived in Queens, so we didn't see each other during the winter. Occasionally we would be at the lake on the same weekend. Ronnie would knock on the back door outside the glassed-in porch, and my heart would skip a beat when I saw him there.

We had lots of fun. We would all go to the First Beach and build a fire by the lagoon at night. There did not seem to be any rules then. Everyone respected our area, and we were cautious about cleaning up and ensuring the fire was completely out. We met at the First Beach during the day. Many of our moms stayed the whole summer with their kids, and mine was one of them. Although the Second Beach was closer to my house, I went to the First Beach.

On the way over, I would often pick up Maureen, whose father was in the FBI, and we were all impressed by that. The next house on the way was Marie Jax, a beautiful and artistic girl who taught us to make scrapbooks using rubber glue. We passed the Sheehy house, but we did not pick boys up—there were three there, and they would eventually show up at the beach. The Hechts' had the home next to the beach, and Howard was always there. Janice and Carol lived near the beach, and Janice and Howie were together. Much later, they married. There was a boy named Lonny. I don't remember where he lived, but he was in love with Marie Jax. He was way more sophisticated than the rest of us.

Ronnie Pederson lived further than the beach, but he always showed up. He was handsome and sweet and fun, and everyone liked him. There were two brothers, the Gandolfos. When their mother, Connie, introduced herself, she always said, "Gan-dolf-o, the Pope lives in my house," referring to Castle Gandolfo, the summer home of the Pope in Italy. Their dad was a jeweler, and Joe, the younger boy, called Junior, made jewelry for all the girls. I still have a small pendant entirely made of dimes. Joe had an older brother named David, who drove a sports car and was called Meatball. He was a football player at St. Johns Prep in Brooklyn. Everyone was crazy about him, but he had a girlfriend named Terry, whom he eventually married. They called their first child Quasimoto.

 Secretly I always loved David, whose father did anything he could to throw us together, and it didn't work. We had a few dates—one to Steeplechase, where we rode the parachute jump. There were many dances at the pavilion and the church in Rocky Point. We always danced together whenever there was an opportunity. Terry did not bother with our bunch, so opportunities came about often. We perfected the Jersey Bounce. With David's strong hands on my waist, I jumped up onto his right hip, took a bounce in the middle, and jumped onto the left hip—he swung me down, and I slid on the floor through his legs, and then he pulled me back, and I jumped up to face him. At Saint Saviour's, we shared a boat trip with a Catholic boys' high school. Luck was shining on me when I heard that we

were joining St. John's Prep. I was a freshman at Saint Saviour's, and David was a senior at St. John's. I found him to show him to my friends, and we performed the Jersey Bounce in front of everyone. People were amazed. I never did that dance with anyone else. David was big and strong, and I knew he wouldn't drop me.

David graduated from St. Johns College and wanted to go to vet school. He went up to Ithaca for an interview. I was serious about Eddie, a freshman at Cornell, so I arranged for David to stay with him in his room. After meeting Eddie, I was no longer in love with David but admired him forever. His father would not pay the vet school tuition when David was accepted. He had majored in chemistry, so it was easy for him to get a job at Domino Sugar. I only saw him once more. He married Terry, and I was engaged to Eddie and teaching first grade. On my way home from work, I saw David outside his house with "Quasi," so I got out of the car, and we visited for a little while and caught up. His brother Joe died when he was only 45, and David went into a deep depression. Terry was prone to depression. Was it contagious? I am pretty sure she thought I was a nuisance.

I had cute boyfriends on and off—they never lasted—and by my Junior year at Port Jefferson, I decided that Eddie was the best, and that was that! I visited him at Cornell when I was at Notre Dame in Baltimore. The bus trip was overnight, and I always arrived bus sick. The fraternity had a lovely English Tudor house, and the top floor was a long, narrow room full of bunk beds. It was cleaned and set aside as a guest room for the girls who came for the party weekends.

My friends are scattered now, but the memories of those summer days remain.

CHAPTER 13

1950 · Peter, Peter le Danseur

 On the third floor above us, there was a family named LiCalzi. They had several boys. Peter was my age, and we became friends. Inside the building, we played some games and danced with Donna. Sometimes, we played outside in the areaway. We went to different schools, and Peter was busy because he was a ballet dancer and had constant rehearsals. One night in his apartment, Peter impressed me tremendously when he showed me how he could stand in the kitchen doorway and slide one leg to the top in a standing split. That night, his parents invited me to Carnegie Hall. I burst into our apartment. "Mom, the best news of all, Peter will dance in Carnegie Hall. His parents invited me to go with them."

We climbed the carved wooden staircase, which was polished so that the ceiling lights danced off them. The thick red carpets added to the exquisite lobby. I knew that I would not forget this day. I was breathless when the heavy curtains parted. The ballet was beautiful, and the music followed me home. I was more impressed with Peter and his poise and grace. He leaped across the stage, spun like a top, and lifted a ballerina, who posed on his shoulder while holding her with one hand!

As we were coming down to Earth, Peter's parents told us there was another surprise. Mr. LiCalzi drove right up to the doors of the Automat for dinner. What a place for fun! They gave us each a batch of quarters and dimes and pointed us toward the long walls. The walls were stainless steel with small doors running up and down. It looked like a ship in a harbor with its lights on. There were names above each wall section to help us navigate. Pies were in one place, cakes nearby, brownies and cookies at the far end. Peter's brother found a heavenly seven-layer chocolate cake. If you lived in Brooklyn, your family often celebrated special days with a Blackout cake from Ebbingers. I can still taste it in my memory. The other spots around the room held free-standing octagons with windows up and down each side. In one of these, I spotted baked beans in a small crock. I was fascinated.

I bought the beans and took them back to the table to be guarded by Peter's parents. Then I ran to the other glass-windowed towers to see what they held. I chose some pie and then some pudding. It was fun to hunt the windows, put in a quarter, and watch them slide open with your prize. When I dropped off my choices, Mrs. LiCalzi advised me to get the main course. I got some pot roast and gravy. Adding green beans made it look like a balanced meal.

I did not know what it was, but it had a huge spoonful of mashed potatoes. I wanted some butter, so Peter's younger brother ran to get it for me. He returned with about five patties, each in a cardboard mini dish. I used it all.

Many years later, I began to attend the ballet regularly in Saratoga, New York. I am often reminded of Peter as he spun in the middle of the stage.

CHAPTER 14

1952 · Garter Belts, Woolies, & Falsies

Until 1940, undergarments for the bottom were called "knickers" for girls. Step-ins came next, and later, "panties" were made of cotton so strong you could boil it.

Thick bands were at the waistline and the legs. Elastic was not available as all the soldiers' uniforms needed it during World War II. After they were worn a few times, the garment would stretch but return to its natural shape when washed, preferably in warm water. On top, children wore t-shirts in a style that is now called a "wife-beater." Socks came next, made of much thinner cotton, and usually turned down at the ankle. Underclothing was not washed every day as it is now. My mother had a washing machine hooked up to the kitchen sink with a hose. It had a feedthrough wringer that squeezed the water out of the garments as she fed them through.

She had to get the article started and then rotate the handle to force it through. The wringer was placed over the kitchen sink, and the water from the piece of clothing in the wringer dropped into the sink. If she dropped the item into the sink, she would have to wring it again. Later, the wringer became electronic, and many children tried to play with it, getting their hands or arms crushed. This was called "Wringer Injury," and it happened often.

During good weather, we dried our clothing outside. Since we lived in an apartment, a "clothesline" went across the yard to the neighbor's apartment on the next street or a tree somewhere. This line was double, running through a wheel. My mom leaned out the window as we lived on the second floor. She hung an item and rolled the clothesline away from herself to make room for the following article. It was a significant problem if she dropped something because we had to go out into the front of our building and through the cellar to get to the backyard. There were demon mice and cockroaches in that cellar, and none of us knew how to turn on the lights.

Wooden clothespins held the clothing tightly to the rope. In a few hours, we would reel it back in. As clothespins were removed, they were put into a bag that closed with a drawstring.

The laundry was placed into a basket to be folded, distributed, or ironed. I remember that my mom had a Coke bottle she filled with water, and it had a cork top with holes in it like a salt shaker. She sprinkled the clothing and rolled it before ironing. If she did not get it all finished, she would put it into the refrigerator until she could get back to it.

In bad weather, there was an interesting device in our kitchen. It was made of metal and could be lowered from the ceiling by a rope and pulley. It had a clothespin bag, and Mom lowered it and pinned the clothing to it as it came out of the wringer. When it was full, she pulled it back up to the ceiling. I can't remember how long it stayed there, but the stove was beneath it, so now I wonder if the clothing smelled like cooking.

We wore uniforms to school consisting of a white blouse with a Peter Pan collar and short sleeves under a blue jumper with a pleated skirt. The blouses were washed once a week unless you spilled something. Everyone had two blouses, but only one jumper. Once a week, my mom put the jumper on the ironing board and sponged spots from it. She pinned the pleats to the ironing board, and when she had four pleats, she covered them with a wet handkerchief and pressed them back into place. They were not washable, and we didn't send things out to be dry-cleaned as we do now.

When we reached the sixth grade, the girls had to wear stockings under the socks. If pantyhose had been invented, life would have been easier. These were not today's silk stockings but made of beige cotton and fastened with a garter belt. The garter belt, which is now considered "sexy," was far from it in the 1940s and quite uncomfortable. It went around your waist and had long pieces of elastic with a hook-on end to hold the stockings. As the socks were not elasticized, they would pull down all day long until the garter belt was lower and lower. It was worn under or over panties. If you wore it under, it would stretch the panty legs out as the day went on. If you wore the garter belt over, the elastic would stretch out as you walked, and you could see the movement through the uniform. My girlfriends and I soon figured this out. We wore one set of panties under and then the garter belt and a second set of panties over. The next day, we would wear the "over" panties next to our skin and keep this system going for one week, in the same manner people used to rotate their bedsheets.

Boys wore the same undershirts, but there is speculation about what they wore next to their skin on the bottom. "Knickers" for boys were not panties but an outer garment buckled at the knee. They wore knee stockings with these. Knickers were held up by suspenders hooked in the same way garter belts did. They wore white cotton shirts and ties on top. In cold weather, a sweater vest went over the white shirt. So far, I have asked four men what they wore for undergarments on the bottom. No one remembers, but they didn't think they wore boxers until they were older. Girls and boys both wore sturdy, tied shoes. Everyone remembers the dog inside the shoe. We listened to the radio every Saturday morning when we ate Cream of Wheat and followed their stories. This is where we first heard the Buster Brown commercial: "I'm Buster Brown, I live in a shoe. That's my dog, Tige, and he lives there too!"

Everyone I knew wore Buster Brown shoes. They also made the Mary Jane patent-leather shoe we got for Easter and wore on Sundays. We were not allowed to wear patent-leather shoes in Catholic school. The nuns thought they reflected your panties! Brown Shoe Company hired dwarfs to play Buster in tours around the United States. These little people, accompanied by a dog, performed in department stores, theaters, and shoe stores from 1904 until 1930. Richard Barker played Buster Brown in many of these Brown Shoe Company advertising campaigns; his story is told in a biography called *Buster Brown and the Cowboy*.* Buster Brown was dressed as a girl or boy. You could choose. He looked more like a cross-dressing pirate, but to a ten-year-old, he was gorgeous. He had a lovely page-boy haircut, a frilly hat, and sturdy shoes. Eventually, the company made sneakers, but our parents thought sneakers were terrible for your feet.

Outer clothing consisted of a coat, usually tweed, which came to the knees. It came with leggings that you pulled on under the uniform skirt when the weather got bad. I was a very feminine little girl, and I did not want to wear leggings. I preferred to freeze. Who knew I would grow up to have horses and spend my life in jeans and chaps?

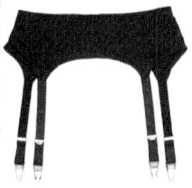 When it began to get cold, probably only 30 degrees in Brooklyn in the 1940s, Mom would say, "Girls, it is time to pull out your 'woolies.'" These were woolen underwear worn over panties that were the length of Bermuda shorts. They itched, and the classroom was warm. I was not too fond of the wooly season. My younger sister reminded me that she would pull down her woolies and pee through her panties during the first wooly days. Now, imagine the layers: panties, garter belts, second pair of panties over the garter belts, and woolies over the panties.

As time went by, satin and silky fabrics were introduced for adult women. No 12-year-old then knew the term "sexy," but what our mothers wore was just that. My mother had full slips with lace decorating the top and the bottom. My aunt wore the half-slip Vassarette and Maidenform advertised as lingerie, and women were thrilled to get it after the war. Bras were satin, and the primary colors for these garments were peach and white; although black was introduced, it was more costly. The girdle, a new instrument of torture, came in all forms.

There were garters to hold up silk stockings. The girdle had several styles: higher waists, natural waist, or a complete one-piece with bras and panties. The panties closed in the crotch with incredible difficulty. The plain girdle was a tube, and panties were worn underneath. Not one person's backside jiggled. Some girdles looked like surgical garments with an extra panel on the front and double hooks. I don't think there were padded bras or push-up bras. Among them, some women like my mother wore "falsies," which were separate pieces of foam rubber shaped like a cone and put into bra cups.

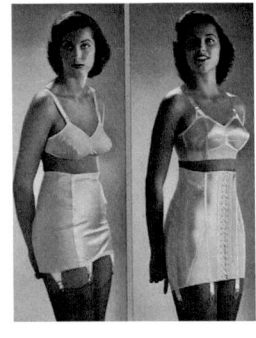 My little sister was begging for ice cream one night, and we did not have any. Daddy announced that he would make her a sundae and went into the kitchen and reappeared with a big smile on his face. My sister was four, and he handed the dish to her. It was a white falsie, and he had put chocolate sauce, some whipped cream, and a cherry on top. It looked exactly like a hot fudge sundae. I think he might have been in trouble with my mom after we went to bed, but we knew what it was, and everyone was laughing.

About 1950, the pointy circular bra was manufactured, the kind Madonna wore at the beginning of her career, and this look lasted for a long while. Meanwhile, teenage girls began to wear crinolines made of horsehair and worn under full skirts topped with Orlon sweaters. It was a matter of status to wear four or five crinolines with a full skirt, bobby socks, and sneakers.

The girdle disappeared for 15- and 16-year-olds who had never liked the squeeze. The heavy cotton panties disappeared, and rayon or nylon replaced these. About this time, they introduced the days-of-the-week panties. One should never wear the Sunday panties on Thursday.

My granddaughters have at least 20 pairs of tiny panties in their dressers, but the littlest one will still dig through to find the ones she likes best. My grandson likes fitted underwear that reaches the thigh. My husband cannot remember what he wore as a boy, and I didn't want to take a census of our men friends, so that information is still to be determined.

The best invention ever was pantyhose. Women happily threw out girdles and garters. The only disappointment is that the whole pair has to go if one leg develops a run. With silk stockings and garter belts, you only lost the stocking with its hole. Women and little girls wear tights in the winter now and would be aghast at the idea of those ugly woolies.

It is my opinion that as women were liberated to work and to speak out, they were also freed from dreadful, ugly, tortuous undergarments.

* Information is taken from Wikipedia

CHAPTER 15

1955 · Daddy's Hat

I would look up and see a hat. When I was a child, men wore three-piece suits, topcoats, and hats in the 1940s. My dad always wore a white shirt and a tie. Once a year, he went to Canal Street and bought a dozen white shirts in a light grayish cardboard box.

The overall color I remember is a combination of gray and brown. Even his ties must have been colorless because I don't recollect any of them. There was a watch chain across his vest, but I don't remember a watch. When I think of his appearance, I see the hat most clearly. If I had to draw him then, I would have made a stick figure with a hat and a huge smile. He must have had unique hats because his name was embroidered in them. My mother disliked one hat, and one day as we were driving across the Brooklyn Bridge, mom reached over, removed the hat, and threw it out the car window.

If there was a fight, I don't remember. Daddy rarely raised his voice to any of us. Two weeks later, a gentleman rang our doorbell and returned the hat. We never knew where he found it, but Daddy was delighted. His embroidered name inside the hat saved the day.

At 21, I saw him from a distance in Baltimore. I returned to the College of Notre Dame from student teaching, and Sister Angela Marie, the Dean of Students, was in front of our dorm with a nicely dressed gentleman. I assumed he was a businessman because the only men on our campus were priests dressed in black robes. My college roommate, Emille, was in the car with me and said, "Robin, I think that is your father." It was.

We found my sister, Janet, who was a year behind me at Notre Dame and went to dinner. He explained that he had just made a stop on a train trip. It was not a surprise to us that our mother wanted a divorce. She had met someone else after 25 years. Daddy did not fly and never traveled unless he drove his car. He was returning from Alabama, where "no-fault" divorces were given. New York State was one of the last to declare "no-fault," but it was not in practice for three more years. To be granted a divorce in New York State meant dragging the family through the courts. Daddy had three daughters to protect, and he was unwilling to do that to us. I know now what it took him to make that trip. I wonder who encouraged him, although my guess would be his sisters. He was the youngest and saw them once a week, and they adored him. I have no memory of how he got home from Baltimore to the end of Long Island that late at night. We must have taken him to the train.

He was despondent, and Janet and I promised he would meet someone else and marry again. He was only 51. Muffin was still living at home, and she was the sweetest and easiest of the three of us. He was not alone, and we would be home for summer. He did remarry, and he was happy again, but he loved my mother until the day he died.

I have movies of him taken in Brooklyn on Third Street, tipping his hat to the camera. I see a happy man who enjoyed life dressed as always in a three-piece suit and a gray felt hat.

At my wedding in 1963, he gave me away, and in that memory, he looks a little like Jiminy Cricket, wearing cutaway and striped trousers, but no hat.

CHAPTER 16

1956 · Football on Long Island Sound

 High school in the 1950s was a time that might never happen again. The girls chose saddle shoes, socks, crinolines, and sweater sets. The boys all wore khaki pants with a belt in the back. There were more "Richie Cunninghams" than "Fonzie's," and almost no one had premarital sex. The birth control pill had yet to be invented.

During the week, you attended class. Many stayed after school for sports or clubs. I took advantage of it as often as I could. The late bus dropped me off at 6:30 p.m. My dinner was always on a plate over a steamer.

Everyone took a bus until they were 16 and then drove. The school was 17 miles from my home. The regular bus ride was interminable, but the late bus was great because all the kids involved in sports were on it. School buses took us to everything. If there was a football or basketball game, the bus picked you up at your house. On the nights of home football games, there was a dance at school called the Zanzibar, and the bus took you to and from school again that night.

If we drew a radius of 20 miles around Port Jefferson, it would include the central school district, which meant that your best friend might live far from you, and mine did. Carol and I were both cheerleaders and would starch and iron our short circular skirts and carry them onto the bus on a hanger—it was really like a badge of honor.

The homecoming game in November 1955 was different and would be an unforgettable memory. It was the first game on the new football field on a hill above the school. I can still smell the Long Island Sound's salt air, and I remember the sunshine reflecting on the water below. The fall colors that year were splendid, with leaves of red and gold. We wore white chrysanthemums on our purple uniform jackets, a gift from the school. The air was crisp and fresh, and the spirit was sky-high. The team looked sharp in their royal purple and white uniforms.

Patchogue High School was the archenemy, and this game was a tradition. We wanted to win, but not just win. We tried to squash them.

On Thanksgiving morning, the coaches reported 2,200 hundred fans in attendance. Parents, students, and alumni crowded in the stands no matter that it was 40 degrees. Frank Sayers ran the opening kickoff back 71 yards for a touchdown, earning him the game's outstanding player. With the Royals off to such a start, Patchogue never had a chance to recover. The coach reported, "Richie Schwender ran down that field like a ballet dancer blocking every Patchogue player."

We were usually excellent hosts, but we weren't so kind to their smug little cheerleaders. I am sure they felt the same way about us. We screamed and jumped and clapped and ran up and down the sidelines. We ran out onto the field for every time-out and did our cheers with the precision that only comes when all six cheerleaders attended practice four times a week after school. Etiquette required that we let the other cheerleading squad run out onto the field first, but we would go anyway if they weren't fast enough. Our advisor would get us later, but we didn't care.

I had very little voice left from screaming, and I wasn't the only one. The players looked like a flock of geese in formation with Frank Sayers at the point. Fans filled the stands, and students were leaning on the brand-new chain-link fence at the side of the field. We stood in front of the bleachers and commanded two hundred people to move in unison, yelling:

LEAN TO THE LEFT!
LEAN TO THE RIGHT!
STAND UP! SIT DOWN!
FIGHT, FIGHT, FIGHT

I don't know where Frank Sayers is now. He would be in his 80s. I wonder how his life has turned out. I am sure he remembers that day as well as I do. He was the hero of the hour, carried on the shoulders of his teammates.

CHAPTER 17

1956 · Keep That Boyfriend

Port Jefferson High School was fabulous in the 1950s. I joined every-thing to make friends, and I did. I became a freshman cheerleader with Carol and Gladys. The following year I ran for class secretary and kept that office until I graduated with Journalism honors. Those four years passed in a blur of boyfriends, girlfriends, school dances, cheerleading, and doing homework but not working too hard. I learned to drive and regained some of the freedom I had lost leaving Brooklyn.

As a Junior, I was appointed editor of the school paper. Juniors worked with the senior editor for a semester. That editor was one of the cutest boys in the school. One sunny day, I saw him standing at the school bus. Of course, I knew him, but there was a connection this time. I decided to marry him, and I chased him shamelessly. We dated and fell in love. He went off to Cornell. The following year, my parents and Eddie dropped me off at Notre Dame of Maryland, back to the nuns. My mother and father were choked up, so Eddie drove the three hours home.

We planned to see each other every seven weeks. I traveled on the overnight bus to Cornell and arrived bus sick. Eddie traveled to Baltimore. On one visit, he parked his car near the YMCA, checked in, dropped his bag, and was back on the street in five minutes. He couldn't find his car and called me. I jumped into a taxi and met him. He had called the police and asked, "Did you tow a vehicle tonight from near the Y?" "No," said the officers. "Then I would like to report a stolen car." "We will be right over." Twenty minutes later, Eddie called again. The officer said, "We were just there; please tell me the street you are on." He gave them the address, and they informed him that there was another Y in the neighborhood, and they would check for him. With an apologetic tone, the officer said, "The village police have towed your vehicle because it was in a no-parking area." We found another cab and asked the driver to take us to the courthouse. Of course, we paid the taxi driver, wiping out my money for the week.

We stopped at the front desk in the courthouse lobby. Turning to Eddie, the policeman said, "The court is upstairs on the left, and the judge will give you a pass to regain your car." Another policeman brought us upstairs and placed us in front of the judge, who wanted to know what had happened. Eddie tried to explain to him about the two different YMCA buildings. The judge, who was not interested, gave him a ticket. We paid the fine and retrieved the car.

This was just the beginning of many experiences trying to keep our seven-week plan.

CHAPTER 18

1957 · Snow, Mountains, Northern Lakes, & Knowing Nothing About Cold

I wanted to be Nancy Drew. She lived alone with her father, and they were always solving a mystery. I wanted my father's attention focused on ME.

But he had my mother and my two sisters. His work took time; his three sisters, my aunts, lived nearby. He also had two brothers, John and Joe. I was disappointed when my father did not attend a horse show where we were competing. We had driven 300 miles, pulling the horse trailer, the horse, and equipment to participate in a show on Long Island. He did not come because his sister, Aunt Gertrude, was hospitalized. My cousin, Patty, told me to read *Blood of My Blood* about the southern Italians and their loyalty to their siblings.

Joe became the patriarch when their father abandoned them and returned to Sicily. He was a dentist and would stuff my mouth with cotton and say, "You are a free patient, no Novocain for you." I thought he did not like me until I spoke to other cousins who received the same treatment.

Our guidance counselor began interviewing students when I was a junior in high school. I thought I would attend a junior college because I knew money was tight and it would only be two years. With no idea about the climate, I had been looking at a beautiful brochure from Vermont's Green Mountain Junior College. I didn't know about snow.

I looked at Oswego on the edge of Lake Ontario. I didn't know about cold.

I had an interview at Cortland Teachers College.

The professor was unpleasant, and the buildings were ugly. I crossed that school out. During this time, I had my father's undivided attention. He drove me all over from Long Island, where we lived. We stayed overnight with relatives. We went out to lunch in each of the cities. I had my first taste of pecan pie in Oswego. Daddy had coconut cream. I remember this as a special time with my father. Whenever I see either of the pies, I envision him sitting across from me in a diner. We returned home, not having made any decisions. Oswego was in the running.

Enter Uncle Joe! For years Daddy, a dental technician, and Uncle Joe had taken care of the School Sisters of Notre Dame, never charging them. These beautiful women had taught them, their siblings, and eventually, all their children at Saint Saviour's in Brooklyn.

Uncle Joe said that the nuns would find a way to help. Daddy was his youngest sibling, and he wanted to be the godfather. He lived in Garden City, and it was on our way, so we picked him up, and my father drove the three hours to Baltimore, where we stayed in a hotel downtown. Uncle Joe had his room, and I shared one with Daddy.

The city was impressive. The houses, referred to as row houses, were all attached. The white steps in front of these houses are well known, and the homeowners scrub and polish them.

We went to a seafood restaurant. Baltimore is built on the shores of the Chesapeake Bay. We had crab, along with every seafood for which Baltimore is known. My father and uncle ate scungilli, an Italian dish of conch or octopus, and neither one appealed to me. I had never even had fish, but Sicily has abundant seafood, and scungilli, pronounced skoon-gilli, is a favorite.

We had an appointment at the College of Notre Dame of Maryland in the morning. The campus was small, and the buildings were lovely, with vine-covered balconies and many trees and paths. It is calm and contained even though it is on North Charles Street, the main thoroughfare.

"We will talk turkey with the nuns," Uncle Joe told me, "and a student will show you around." A student appeared, and she was cute and friendly and from the deep south. While Daddy and Uncle Joe spent time with the nuns in a small office next to a beautiful formal lounge, I saw the campus and the beautiful dorm rooms. Most girls I met wore plaid, pleated skirts, sweaters, knee socks, and penny loafers, and no pants or jeans were allowed.

"Are you applying for next year?" they asked.

"I like everything I have seen," I said, realizing I meant it.

Baltimore is warmer than New York, but the weather can change in a minute. Good weather was a huge plus after the cold climate schools I had seen already. My guide brought me back to visit with Sister Cora Lee and Sister Angela Marie. I remembered every rule my mother had ever taught me. I answered their questions enthusiastically.

They were proud that Notre Dame was the oldest Catholic college for women in America. I left with a catalog and an application, which I sent in immediately.

A few weeks later, I received a thick envelope and was accepted! The cost was $1,200 a year, and they offered me a $300 scholarship and a $300 assistantship.

I loved my years and my friends at Notre Dame. I graduated in 1962 with a BA in Elementary Education and earned the entire investment back in my first year of teaching.

CHAPTER 19

1957 · Dancing in the Gym

The loud music from the gym encouraged me to move faster through the high school building. The rhythm had me dancing down the stairs to the first floor and the gym. Everyone dances in pairs of two girls, one girl, and one boy. Two boys never danced together in the 1950s. Rock around the clock was playing, and when it stopped, most kids walked back to the bleachers. A few couples leaned against the gym wall between dances, holding hands. I was 16 and a junior at Port Jefferson High School. I had moved here from Brooklyn when I was 14 and a freshman and learned to fit into a very different environment. I came from eight years of Catholic school where children obeyed the rules and moved in straight lines. No talking was allowed in the halls or the classroom. This considerable difference was not difficult, but just not what I had known. In psychology class, Mr. Wenburg asked a question. I raised my hand, and he called on me. I stood next to my desk to answer, and some kids laughed. Mr. Wenberg ignored them and asked me if I had just come from a Catholic school. Then he explained to the class that students showed respect for the nuns by standing to answer a question.

Once I got the idea of public school, I made a place for myself. I was a class officer and a JV cheerleader, and I had many new friends. I had my eye on a boy who was a senior and a basketball player. He was adorable, and he was in the National Honor Society and very well-liked. He was tall and blond and had no idea how cute he was.

Still hurrying, I walked into the gym, and there he was.

"Want to dance?" "Sure," I answered, giving him a sunny smile. He headed to the wall when the music ended and still had my hand. I was surprised and pleased. The students who had graduated from Port Jeff sent banners back when they arrived at college to begin their new lives. The gym looked huge, with a stage on one side and bleachers on the other. College banners covered the rest of the wall space. We were standing between some couples who were quite serious about their relationship. One great-looking girl named Judy had a perfect blonde pageboy. She was standing with her boyfriend, and they had been a couple since Freshman year. Judy was going to nursing school. I imagined her beautiful appearance in her starched white uniform and nurse's cap. We all thought that this couple would marry after college, but Judy went to nursing school and married a doctor, leaving the high school boyfriend behind, and he never got over it.

Rolinda wore a dark green sweater and a green corduroy full skirt over five crinolines. She had slept overnight at my house the night before and wore my green outfit that all the girls loved. We shared our clothing, lending it to any friend. After wearing a uniform for eight years in Catholic school, I was crazy about clothes. I was wearing a straight brown skirt with my beige sweater.

The best days were the day before a game when we wore our cheerleading uniforms to school to whip up excitement. Too soon, the bell rang, and the hour of dancing in the gym ended. We had a very long school day because we all traveled by bus. The buses made two trips—one to take elementary school children home and then back for the high school students.

Dancing days were not always smooth. One day I borrowed a friend's football sweater and wore it all day, and Eddie never asked me to dance. Blair was a kicker on the football team known as Golden Toe Marelli, and Gladys was his girlfriend. They have been married for 60 years. Eddie asked me to dance the next day, and we leaned on the wall. I wasn't about to let him slide away from me, not just at the gym wall. I asked a friend, Will, if we could share lockers. I would love to have a first-floor locker. Mine was on the second floor, where Will had several classes, and Will's locker was next to Eddie's. None of them got it, but now I managed to be there between classes.

We lived in a very rural area, and I did not drive yet. Once I asked a very popular boy named Botch to drive me to a party at Irene's house, a beautiful Victorian on at least 500 acres of land. Her parents had emigrated from Poland and were very successful farmers. Eddie and I sat in the corner of this house on the floor in front of a bay window. Everywhere he was, I often appeared; I chased him shamelessly. By the time he left for Cornell at the end of the summer, I knew I would miss him terribly. I wrote faithfully, telling him all that was happening in our school.

I had a fantastic senior year and attended all the parties, but I never dated anyone else. When Eddie came home, we had a great summer. He worked as a waterfront director at a Boy Scout camp five miles from my house. Several nights a week, I would pick him up at the camp's back entrance and bring him over. My parents loved him.

In September, we parted again; I was off to Notre Dame of Maryland in Baltimore. We planned to meet at Grand Central and take the Long Island Railroad home together to our separate stops, and our parents looked forward to picking us up. As I was looking for him, a woman stepped in front of me, and I said, "Excuse me?" Not focusing on this woman, I stepped aside. She moved with me, and I looked up to see that it was Eddie's mother. His parents had decided to pick him up at Grand Central as a surprise. Our plan for the train was not mentioned. They took us to their house, where we ate pizza, and then he took his father's car and drove me home. My mother was furious. I said when I called her to say I was at his house, "Oh, I am so happy to be home for Thanksgiving." She said in a cold voice that only she could do, "But, darling, you are not home yet!"

Eddie graduated a year before me and went to Cornell Medical School, New York City. When I finished school, I took a teaching job on Long Island and lived at home. We had become engaged, and I brought my wedding planner into focus. By then, I was an expert. We have been very happily married since 1963. You do the math!

CHAPTER 20

1958 · A Sister on Point

"Do you want to come over to my house for Sunday dinner tomorrow? I want you to meet my sister. She keeps asking me questions about my new girlfriend," Eddie asked on the phone.

"Sure, I said. Since it is daytime, I will drive over by myself."
"That is great. Come at 1:00."

He lived twenty miles away, so I would leave at 12:20 to be sure. I wore a lime green circular skirt with three crinolines and a dark green sweater, no makeup, that would come later.

 Helene was so young, the same age as my youngest sister at fourteen. She always sat with her toes pointed since she was a ballet student. She was friendly and sweet; we got along immediately. Still, in middle school, she had not dated yet.

Several years later, when she did begin to date, her  father and her brother would stand behind the door with baseball bats as the poor boy entered, then they would laugh and say it was just a joke. Helene did not think it was funny.

She was still very interested in ballet. A recital was coming up, and she invited me. It was amazing. She danced on point, holding a large ring of roses over her head.

At dinner, after the performances, she let Eddie finish her Sundae. It seems this was a constant occurrence. They got along beautifully. She always played a part in his games.

After several years of dating, I often stayed overnight at Eddie's house because we lived so far apart. At that time, Port Jefferson was a central high school. By the time Helene went, Sachem High School had opened in Lake Ronkonkoma. When I stayed overnight, I slept with her in her 3/4 bed.

 In my senior year, I broke my ankle. When Eddie came home from school for the holiday, I stayed overnight, wearing my walking cast. The one thing she will often remind me of is how worried she was that I would kick her with my cast.

When Helene began to look at colleges, she came to Notre Dame and spent a night. After visiting me for a weekend in Baltimore, she chose to attend Notre Dame.

We are more like sisters than sisters-in-law. My sister, Janet, was at Notre Dame with Helene. We were bridesmaids in each other's weddings, Godparents for our children, and we have grown old together with friendship and love.

CHAPTER 21

1958 · Hi, I'm Robin

The year was 1958, and the place was the College of Notre Dame of Maryland, the oldest Catholic college for women in America. The school sisters of Notre Dame were delighted with the number of applications they had received for the class of 1962. They over-booked our first-year class. Consequently, our rooms were set up for four. Originally, they were for two. Several parents were there as well. My roommate, Emille, will tell you that I jumped into the doorway with a tennis racket and said, "Hi, I'm Robin!"

I was the last to arrive and did not have a tennis racket, but I am sometimes enthusiastic. At least eight people were jammed into a suite with one bathroom between two bedrooms. The suite with one bathroom would have been lovely for four women. But this room had four beds, four desks, and three dressers. Add to this several sets of parents.

Since I was the last to arrive, I got a top bunk and a bottom drawer in each dresser. We shipped our trunks to the school in those days, and they had been put into the basement. After locating my trunk, I found a shopping cart to move what we unpacked to take up to our rooms. There was one elevator. When we returned upstairs, I saw nine faces: three pretty roommates and six parents. We entered the room, trying to get to the dressers. Looks from my new friends immediately fixed on Eddie, a 6'3" handsome medical student. They thought he was my brother. I quickly set them straight, introducing him and explaining that he had come to help me.

"What a great boyfriend," said Oonah Buckley, a blue-eyed blonde who introduced us to her parents, Patrick, and Moira. At the sound of the Irish brogue, I looked at my mom and saw tears in her eyes.

Carmen Inez, a tall, dark-haired girl, oozed warmth and had a contagious laugh. The family lived in Puerto Rico; her mother did not accompany them, but her father, Luis, was gregarious and spoke with everyone. Emille Franklin introduced a sparkly father, Rafael, and her mom, Maruca, who had the most beautiful thick hair. I did not know then that Emille and I would be roommates for the entire four years and friends for life.

How would this work with such limited space? I had to find a place to put my hanging clothes. All the closets were full, and I had to take a tiny makeshift place in the runway between the two sinks, which eight women would use. We later discovered that we were assigned by alphabetical order, which is incredible how well that worked. Emile and Carmen were cousins from Puerto Rico, which explained their beautiful hair. Oonah was the epitome of an Irish maiden. She was what the Irish called "FEY." She spoke very softly, almost in a whisper.

With everything accomplished, our families began to leave. My parents were upset as I was the first child to leave home, so Eddie was driving. I went up the back staircase, trying to hide my tears. As we waved goodbye to our families, we worried about how we would all get along as roommates in such tight quarters.

We did!

CHAPTER 22

1958 · The Wedding Planner

I married my high school boyfriend, so this was a wedding in the planning for six years. I had dreamed of my wedding since I attended my first one at 12.

Never mind the cost, I knew what I wanted! I wanted this groom I found at age 17 in the high school parking lot, waiting for the school bus. I had a few boyfriends, so it wasn't love at first sight, but "Wow, he would make a good boyfriend. I think I will make that happen." And make it happen, I did! Eddie Kappler was a senior and determined to go to college free, so it took work. I managed to be everywhere he was. He was a basketball player, and I was a cheerleader. Our squad did individual cheers when the team member made a basket, and I decreed that I was the only one to do the personal cheer for Eddie Kappler. If there was a party I knew he would attend, I would manage to get there. I begged my friend, Will, to let me share his locker as it was next to Eddie's. I lived far out in the boondocks. Once, I paid a friend of his $1 to pick me up and drive me to a party I knew he was attending. It was the best dollar I ever spent.

About two weeks later, he came to a party at my house. He told me he was planning to go to college without any ties to a girlfriend and that I should date Dan, a boy in my class who was my friend but would have liked to be something more. My husband of 50 years likes to tell new friends about that evening. I said, "I do not want to date Dan, I want to date you, and I always get what I want." A week later, he asked me out, and that was that. Well, not quite so easily.

It was April 1957 when we began to date, and we went to all school functions together and danced in the gym at lunchtime. It was the Fabulous Fifties. Our school day was very long because the buses had to be used for the elementary schools and then return to the high school. Classes started at 8:15 a.m., and the buses returned at 4:15 p.m. to take us home. Dancing was held in the gym during the fifth period to break up the long day and give the students a social hour. Most of us worked it out to have fourth-period lunch, so we had an entire hour in the gym. Girls would begin by dancing together, and then the boys, sitting in the bleachers, would cut in. If you had a serious relationship, you leaned against the wall between songs. Eddie and I spent many hours leaning on that wall for April, May, and June. By May, he had asked me to the prom.

That summer, Eddie worked as a waterfront director at a Boy Scout camp near my house. I could finally drive and pick him up in the evening and bring him to my home, where I would have chocolate chip cookies or brownies waiting. My family was also crazy about him; he paid attention to my younger sisters, who adored him. Now that we were a couple, I wanted to go steady, but he did not want to give me his ring. Like many friends, I wanted to wear it on a chain around my neck.

Eddie said at a beach party one night, "Would you go behind that rock with me? I have something for you." The ring, I knew it! I jumped up from the sand, and we left the fire and our group to go behind the rock. He had his hand closed over something and gave me a piece of phosphorous. When I looked at it, I expected the ring, but I exclaimed how beautiful it was, glowing in the dark.

When the summer of 1957 ended, I was back at Port Jefferson High School, and he was off to Cornell. We had agreed that we would or could date other people, but we had something serious. He was too busy as a pre-med student and did not date much. He joined a fraternity, Theta XI, and when people asked him his name, he said "Gus." Technically his name is Gustav Edward Kappler III, but his mother did not like the name Gus and under pressure from the family, she used the name but agreed that he would be called Eddie. His friends from Cornell call him Gus, and I call him Eddie, as do our pre-1957 friends.

His fraternity had its first big party, and he invited me to come for the weekend. We had spent time together at Thanksgiving and Christmas and had celebrated New Year's Eve with high school friends, so this would be my first time visiting Cornell. The party was formal, so I mailed my gown to him, and I looked forward to taking the train. It snowed on the morning of my trip, and we had a car accident on the way to the station. I spent the following week in the hospital with a broken leg and missed our college weekend. It would be spring break before I would see him again, but our summer was something to look forward to, and he would be working at camp again, allowing us to see each other most nights.

In the fall of 1958, we left for school in opposite directions. He went back to Cornell, and I went to Notre Dame of Maryland. I did date a little but looked forward to the weekends we would see each other. We managed every seven weeks for the next four years. It was a long trip between Ithaca and Baltimore. Meanwhile, friends were getting engaged and married, and I kept notes in my head about a wedding.

I would take the bus from Baltimore to Ithaca, leaving at night and arriving in the morning. I was scared most of the trip, holding my purse close. The bus stopped in Wilkes Barre, Pennsylvania, for a half hour, and then I changed buses. Knowing I was on the last leg, I finally slept, and the motion sickness disappeared.

By Eddie's junior year in 1960, he broke down and gave me his fraternity pin. We knew we weren't interested in dating other people, and we were both very involved in school. He was studying for the medical college application tests, and I was happy to see him every seven weeks, so dating other people was over. I had enough social life with my girlfriends, most of whom planned their weddings for the summer after graduation. There were *Brides* magazines everywhere, and we all read them faithfully. I remember one ad showing sheets and bedspreads, saying: "Don't just make a bed, decorate it." One evening three friends came into my room. They had been downtown in Baltimore for the day and said, "We chose your china and crystal for you in a jewelry store downtown. We want to take you tomorrow to see it." The next day we took the bus into Baltimore, and sure enough, these three friends, who knew I loved lavender and purple, had found the perfect place settings for me. I began to collect brochures of things I would want for wedding presents. There were still three years left until we would marry.

During one of our summer dates in 1960, we went to see *An Affair to Remember* with another couple. Chris had a Nash Rambler, famous because the seats folded down and made a bed. The four of us were sitting in the back with our feet stretched out on this bed and food laid out like a picnic. As Cary Grant and Deborah Kerr made a date to meet each other a year later, Eddie whispered to me. "We can make a date for our wedding. How about June 20, 1963?" That was my only proposal. He figured out the time, and we were married on June 29, 1963.

Eddie had $300 to spend, and we drove into New York to the diamond center, where he bought me a ¾ carat diamond ring. He gave it to me at Saint Patrick's Cathedral at the altar of Saint Elizabeth, the patron saint of patience.

My father allowed me to take a car back to Baltimore because I was student teaching. Eddie was in New York City, so we saw each other once a month. I graduated from college in 1962 and worked for a year, teaching first grade. I was living at home and saving every penny I could. I made my wedding dress, first out of sheets and then silk. My mother made the bridesmaids' dresses. I had decided on an all-white wedding that had impressed me the year before. My friends gave showers and luncheons, and I held a tea party to display my gifts. I tried different hairstyles and headpieces until I was satisfied. We met with the priest when we could squeeze in a weekend away from med school. Etiquette decreed that the men should wear cutaways because we were being married at a mass at 11:00 a.m. I planned and purchased the flowers, decided on the meal, and addressed the invitations as if it was second nature. It had been in my head for six years, waiting to be carried out.

The night before the wedding, someone left the window open in my bedroom. We were all on the patio at my father's house for the rehearsal dinner, a cookout. Long Island in June can be lovely, and it was a beautiful evening. I walked into my room to check how I looked and began screaming as I saw that hundreds of gigantic brown crunchy June bugs had flown in through the open window and were resting all over my dress! Calming myself, I opened the back door saying, "Daddy, please come in here and help me!" My father was a very relaxed soul who never knew a moment of panic. He got the Electrolux, attached the hose, and vacuumed the June bugs away.

Five white cars with purple ribbons streaming from the antennae, lined up in front of our house to drive the bridesmaids to the church. There was no money for limos, and this worked as well. My dad drove me in his white car.

My first-grade class attended the wedding, and I had my picture taken with them in the back of the church. The mass was beautiful but long and warm in the church. We were kneeling throughout because *Brides* magazine advised that this presented the prettiest view of the back of the dress. I thought I would faint at one point, and Eddie looked at me and whispered, "Take a deep breath. You are okay." This set the tone for the rest of our lives. No matter what tragedies we have endured, he has always given me that sense of security that everything would be okay.

The June bugs were not the end of the things that could go wrong. After the mass, my dad drove the car with the newly married couple. I leaned forward in the backseat to tell him something, and the zipper on my dress split open! "It's okay," I said, "this was advertised as a self-healing zipper." So my new groom zipped it down and back up, and it worked.

I had hired a top-rated band, led by Tony DiMartino, our area's best wedding band leader. When we arrived at the venue for the reception, a young woman approached me and said, "I am Angela DiMartino. My dad had a car accident, and I am filling in for him. I plan to introduce the bridal party one couple at a time. I have the list. They will form an arch with their flowers. You will enter under the arch after the best man and maid of honor. The name is Viverito, right?" I said, "Yes" and "okay," and she left. I had only been married for an hour. Of course, my new name was Kappler, but it hadn't registered. The bridal party entered the ballroom two at a time, and following a loud fanfare, Angela DiMartino spoke, "Ladies and gentlemen," she said, "please welcome the bride and groom, for the very first time as a married couple..."

MR. and MRS. VIVERITO

And that is how we started our marriage.

CHAPTER 23

1958 · To Our Eyes Will E'er Bring Tears

Graduation at Port Jefferson High School was held in front of the glass wall on the beautiful patio outside the cafeteria. This platform was large enough for a class of 300 who looked stunning in their royal purple caps and gowns. The ceremony was held outdoors on a lovely day in June, a perfect setting with a tree-lined street to the left and the school facing a green field that had once been used for football games.

Port Jefferson's traditional daisy chain had always been woven the day before graduation. Thousands of daisies and greens were delivered to the school, and several teachers showed the junior class members how to incorporate their leaves into a substantial chain. The goal was to weave two chains 12 inches in diameter and at least 100 feet long to be carried on the shoulders of the Junior class as a passage for the Seniors. The band played joyful songs of celebration.

As class officers Rolinda and I had the honor of leading the daisy chain one on each side. The girls wore gowns, and the boys wore jackets and ties. The seniors walked through this honor guard to the stage as parents and friends held back tears. Awards were announced, and each student walked up to the podium to receive their diploma enclosed in a purple leather folder. The ceremony ended with youthful voices singing:

> "The sight of Royal Purple to our eyes will e'er bring tears
> As we think of Port Jeff High School
> And our friends of former years"

1959 · A Cup of Tea & a Strawberry Pie

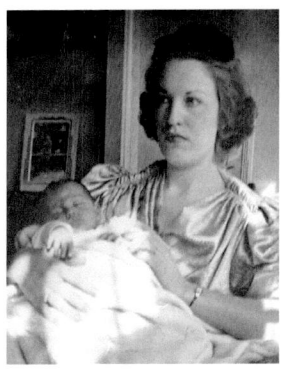 

When I was born, my father made a wooden scrapbook for my pho-tos and carved "The Golden Child" on the front. I always believed it. He could make us each feel we were his favorite daughter.

Eventually, I had to give up the position as the ONLY CHILD; my sister Janet was born. My mom heard me comforting my new sister, who was in a crib in what had been my room, which I had not shared until now. She heard me saying in a sing-song tone, "Don't cry, baby, don't cry." Finally, she decided to help me with the crying infant and tiptoed into the room to find me standing on a chair over the crib, slapping my new sister, and crooning to her in time with the blows. Why was I hitting her? I have no idea. Jealousy at two is not difficult to believe when looking at sibling rivalry. I am the firstborn.

We had a long hallway in our apartment, and my dad would invite the other toddlers in the building to come over and watch cartoons, which he showed on a 16mm movie camera. He lined the chairs up in a single file row down the hallway, and we were all very excited to be at the "movies." During one session, a child coughed, and my dad turned on the lights and said, "Who coughed?" The offending child was escorted back to his apartment. Later, I asked why he took the boy home. Daddy said, "I don't want you to catch his cough!" reinforcing that my health was more important than anyone else's.

Eventually, there was a third child, but at five, I thought she was my doll, brought home for me as a toy. At first, she was petite and was named Carolyn; the nurse commented to my mother, "She is as big as a muffin. I could eat her in one bite." Nearing seventy-five, she is still called Muffin, and the next generations of children call her Aunt Muffin. When she attends a bridal shower, she gives everyone muffin tins, mixes, bowls, and spatulas.

As children, my middle sister, Janet, and I often fought because she tried to step into what I considered my age group. I can remember complaining that she was always following me. I resented it when privileges given to me as the oldest were also given to her. The first time I was allowed to wear nylons, so was she. When I was permitted to ride my bicycle in the city, Janet gave me a smug look when they said she could do the same. Instead of enjoying these things together, I thought the privileges should be mine, and she should wait out the two-year difference. The worst thing was that my mother, an excellent seamstress, dressed us alike!

When we were young, we played well at home, sharing toys, reading, and listening to the radio. We had a table and chairs in our oversized bedroom. We ate cream of wheat on Saturday mornings while listening to the morning shows. I recently bought tapes of many of these shows, and we shared them, listening to them this time in our cars. Our favorites were *Digger Odell, the Friendly Undertaker,* and *Let's Pretend.*

I liked to make breakfast for all of us. I made chocolate pudding on the gas stove, and we ate it warm with a soup spoon. Sometimes we made pudding cakes layered with graham crackers. Perhaps we were inventing the graham cracker crust. We also enjoyed the graham crackers soaked in milk with sugar on the top.

 There is something about siblings sharing a joke. In church one Christmas Eve, we sat behind a woman with a long feather protruding from her hat's right side. It kept hitting her husband as she moved her head. He would swat it away, and she was completely unaware of this. We three looked at each other and began to laugh. We received a few dirty looks, and it got worse. We could not stop until our mother gave us "the look." Then, we had stifled giggles that returned through the mass.

My sisters don't mind making fun of me and reminding me of my officious actions. My youngest sister was waiting in line for a movie with a group of friends. On my way to my senior prom, I saw her smoking in the movie line. I made my boyfriend stop the car. I jumped out and walked over to her in my prom regalia, took the cigarette from her mouth, stamped it out, and said, "Ladies, do NOT smoke on the street!" Everyone looked at her and said, "That is my older sister. She does things like that!"

Another time, I baked a strawberry pie from scratch. I must have missed an ingredient because it did not gel. My boyfriend, whom I later married, was coming over, and this was to be our treat after a barbecue. When I put the pie in front of them and tried to cut it, a delicious runny mess presented itself. I served it with spoons and added a can of Reddi Whip to the table. Why did I not know better? The three began to put the strawberry glue on their spoons, cover it with whipped cream, and then shoot it at each other. I never joined in horseplay. I was meticulous about my appearance and hair, and I had to leave the table for fear they would get some of it on me. I realized that I had no more power that day because I couldn't make them stop. They were hysterical and could not have stopped if they wanted to. The pie incident foreshadowed my husband's ability to join forces with them as another sibling, mainly when the joke was on me.

Today we rarely fight or even argue. My youngest sister is the nicest woman in America, and I doubt she would act disagreeably with anyone. While traveling together in London, my middle sister and I disagreed over which bus route to take. She said, "Why is it that you never trust my directions? If I say the green route, you think it is the red route!" "Fine," I reply, "I will not speak to you for the rest of the day." "That works for me," she retorted. The silence lasted all ten minutes, and then we laughed about it. Her directions were the correct ones.

I grew up to be active, holding class offices and chairing committees. After college, I became involved in national organizations. I worked hard and often became president. I served on boards and ran fundraisers, successfully building a gigantic committee pulling our town library out of a financial hole and into the eyes of the citizens of our community. We had fun, I made many new friends, and gained the respect of local business leaders. Being the oldest child makes one feel responsible for those around them. Fortunately, my sisters accept my wish to be in charge, and they slide around it.

 Our hearing is not what it used to be as we get older. We don't hear each other well. We share a particular joke about three sisters standing on a corner, which epitomizes our birth order.

The first sister says, "It is windy!"

The second sister replies, "No, it is Thursday."

Quite agreeably, the third sister smiles and says,

"So am I. Let's go have a cup of tea."

CHAPTER 25

1955 · Talismans, Amulets, & Uniforms

I understood the power of a talisman long before I knew the word. My skate key hung around my neck on a ribbon every sunny day after school. Our skates had ball-bearing wheels, and they fit over shoes or sneakers with a toe piece that locked into the front of the foot and a strap around the ankle. The center of the skate was a slide so that they were "one size fits all." Anyone can use a skate key to change the skate's size, add or remove the wheels if needed, or tighten the toe piece. Smaller children were fitted by their moms, who then stayed on the stoop to watch the children skate in the street. Instead of returning to their moms, the children would ask me to adjust a skate for them. Before long, I felt like the chief of the skaters, an important role.

Catholic kids had crosses or crucifixes on chains around their necks. Jewish children wore the star of David or the Chai, outward signs of who they were. The miraculous medal was very special to the Catholic girls, and the St. Christopher medal to the boys.

In ancient times, the talisman was thought to ward off evil. Women wore charms like bear claws and lion's teeth, called amulets. The cave people believed an amulet had magic protective power. Eddie, my husband, saw extraordinary proof in Vietnam's operating room when a young soldier was shot. The St. Christopher medal was bent by a bullet that would have otherwise hit the young man's heart.

People had St. Christopher medals in their cars. There are many stories about the medal saving lives. One of my favorite photos is of a well-dented St. Christopher medal. Two soldiers were in their hooch in Phu Bai, Vietnam, consuming a case of beer. One aimed a pistol at his friend, assuming it was unloaded in a foolish act. He pulled the trigger! The young soldier was rushed to the base hospital with an apparent abdominal bullet wound and blood loss. At surgery, his liver and stomach were repaired. Not only was the bullet retrieved but also a deformed St. Christopher's medal. It had deflected the bullet away from his heart into his abdomen, saving his life. Time passed, and the talismans were added. Girl Scout badges could be sewn onto banners that girls wore like Miss America pageant contestants. The boys had their badges sewn directly onto their uniform shirts. In high school, letter sweaters announced a position! They were usually cardigans with pockets.

Second to the skate key was a megaphone charm that I wore around my neck on a chain. That was only replaced or added to by wearing your boyfriend's school ring on a ribbon, declaring that you were going steady. My husband, who was also my boyfriend in high school, would never give me his school ring. One night, we were at a beach party on the Long Island Sound with about twenty friends. He said quietly, "Come behind that rock with me. I have something special." *'Here it comes; he is going to give me his ring.'* I rushed behind the rock, and he opened his hand to show me a piece of phosphorous and explained why it was shining in the dark.

I never got that ring. It is in his jewelry box in our bedroom sixty years later, but I am no longer interested in wearing it.

I find uniforms exciting. We had to wear tiny jumpsuits in navy blue in high school gym class. They were pretty cute, but there was something better worn by the members of the Girls Leaders Club. We all loved the white one-piece outfits with skirts and bloomers. Once I saw them, I signed up for every inter-mural team, and pretty soon, I was tapped for Leader's Club and the white uniform. We took attendance in gym class, and I think that was all. As a cheerleader, I had a second uniform and was proud to wear my cheerleading skirt and top. On Fridays, before a game, we would wear our uniforms all day in school before a pep rally. It made me feel very special.

The college years brought the possibility of pins and rings. Our college ring had a miraculous medal embedded inside and the year on the outside. I wore this every day in college and for many years afterward until it would no longer fit over my arthritic knuckles. No jeweler wants to make it more prominent because they are afraid they will ruin the miraculous medal embedded in plastic on the inside. Then the other rings were the diamonds, but getting pinned was the first step. From the day my boyfriend got his fraternity pin, I dreamed of him giving it to me. I wanted to be "pinned," but I was in Baltimore, and he was in Ithaca. He was pre-med, which left time only for studying and fraternity parties, where I am sure he met plenty of girls, but you did not have to call that a date. By my junior year in college, he gave in, and we were pinned, as were many of my friends at school. No more dating other people after that. Married and in medical school when we all reached age twenty-one, and it was the first time we could vote. I think we registered right there. One of the guys in Eddie's class showed up wearing the white uniform that third-year students wore in the hospital only but not out on the streets. We were all in the gym of the nearby elementary school to vote. Enter John Smythe, in his white uniform and carrying his laminated diploma from Yale to prove literacy!

Seven years later, Eddie was serving in Vietnam. Physicians enter the army as majors. They have the coveted oak leaves on their uniforms, as other amulets are often a point of contention with the enlisted men. Doctors were majors immediately. Eddie was in Saigon with three different doctors, and all were taking their Medical Boards. When the boards were over, they celebrated together and got pretty smashed. The MPs stopped them, and when they were finally released, they asked the MPs, "Why did you stop us?" and one replied, "Frankly, Sirs, you don't look old enough to be majors."

My father-in-law, an outstanding athlete at Cornell, was 'A Wearer of the C', signifying that he had played on several varsity teams and was captain of at least one. They were given gold charms with a red C in the center. These were given to our daughter, Kim, when she was a freshman at Cornell. She put the charm on a chain and wore it to class and parties, proclaiming her heritage.

Talismans are described as objects thought to have magical powers and to bring good luck. An amulet is an ornament also believed to protect.

CHAPTER 26

1956–1970 · What Will I Be?

 My Italian father had often said, "You don't need a college degree to get married and raise children, but if you are determined, then I think you should be a teacher or a nurse." I am pretty sure this was the common mantra of middle-class fathers in the nineteen fifties. His philosophy restricted my choices as I wanted to be a social worker. Mommy put her head in the door, and she also had advice, "Robin, your Daddy is right. It's not a good idea to deal with things that make you sad. You wear your heart on your sleeve, and you will bring the problems home with you. Look for a happy career." My boyfriend, whom I would later marry, told me that the person he remembered most was his fourth-grade teacher, so I entered the education department, which turned out to be the right place for me. The department head, Sister Immaculata, had just been appointed. She wasn't much older than we were, and she was delightful, kind, and completely innocent. Dressed in the black and white habit of the School Sisters of Notre Dame, she wore black heeled lace-up shoes on her tiny feet. Some women in our class nicknamed her *'Goody Two Shoes'* after a children's book about a virtuous little girl.

While our classmates were reading French literature, working on the permutation of Latin squares, experimenting in the chemistry labs, or writing poetry with the famous Sister Maura, we were going through our reading lists. *Wind in the Willows* was a favorite. We studied the Newberry and Caldecott prize winners; *Make Way for Ducklings* was a favorite too. In junior year, we observed teachers in local schools every Tuesday. We were guests in classrooms decorated with fabulous bulletin boards and teachers who were excited about their jobs and had the children enthusiastic about teaching. I couldn't wait to get to my class. When we visited a school for observation, we learned to lead thirty children by singing "B-I-N-G-O; Bingo is my name-O."

In senior year, we became student teachers and were off on our own to different parts of Baltimore. My first student teaching experience was in a sixth-grade class, and my supervising teacher said, "I don't believe in babying you. My idea is to throw the student-teacher into cold water and let her sink or swim." Exuberant would have been a good description of her thirty students. Mrs. Bocek never taught me how to maintain discipline, and these kids were out of control. I almost sank. I began to have chest pain so horrible that Eddie asked a physician he knew to see me when I was visiting during spring break. This young doctor performed tests and then asked if I had a new job. "This usually manifests itself when people encounter stress in their lives." He gave me some medication to take at dinner time, and the chest pains went away, but I never controlled that sixth grade. I was suffering from a phenomenon called Globus Hystericus, a perfect name for what I was feeling. When I got back to school, my roommate Emille started laughing. "That is what they give the old ladies in Puerto Rico." I didn't care, and it worked for this young lady.

The second semester of student teaching was my reward for having survived Mrs. Bocek. Our director at Notre Dame, Miss

Trueschler, took pity on me. She observed us in class from time to time and decided that I needed a break after the challenging sixth-grade experience. She assigned me to an excellent first-grade teacher in Baltimore's lower-income area, and again, I decided that I would love teaching.

The children were making a map of their school area. Mrs. Redifer had made a pattern of a child, and together we cut them out and gave them to the children to fill in their appearance and create a miniature of themselves. I had to control my laughter when I saw how cute these were and how some of them captured their look. They tacked them up on the streets we had drawn, placing their little people walking to school. When we finished the project, I asked, "Who would like the honor of placing this American flag on the roof of our school?" One little girl jumped up and spoke. "I would!" And she did. As she walked proudly back to her place, I asked the children, "What does our flag mean?" A chubby little boy called out, "It means we don't allow no Katliks in here." The answer had surprised me; however, Mrs. Redifer smiled at me and nodded her head to go on. It was not a religious lesson, so I asked if anyone had a better answer, and I got one.

The teachers and principal were young professionals that I could identify with, and many helped me with problem-solving. There were some adorable experiences in this classroom. I had a dream job with everything a first grader or a teacher could want to use. I acquired two painting easels and placed them in the back of the room.

When children finished their work, I often let them put on the plastic apron and paint for fifteen minutes. I often scolded one naughty boy named Arthur for shouting out; he was told to sit at the back table for a time-out.

I taught in groups for reading, and while one group was reading in a circle with me, the others had paperwork to do, involving cutting and pasting. They had to match words with pictures; they loved this work and were very quiet. I became engrossed in the reading group at the front of the room. Everything was tranquil until Dora screamed. Arthur had painted his hands green. I took him by the shoulders and walked him back to the sink to clean him up. After that, I kept the child in time-out in the front of the room. Denny Dimwit, with his hat and his stool, was a pretty good idea, albeit probably illegal now.

A charming black boy had broken his arm or shoulder. The cast was set at a right angle to his body, straight out from his side. Donna raised her hand when I lined the children up to go to the lavatory. "Miss Viverito," she said, "I am worried about how the colored boy will go to the bathroom." With a six-year-old's innocence, another small boy answered her, "I am his friend, so I can help him."

At the end of that school year, I got married, and most of my students came to church for the wedding. My album has a photo of me with these little people in the back of the church. I moved to New York City, where my next job was in Spanish Harlem. After taking an exam and being granted a license, the New York City School District placed new teachers in areas easily accessible by public transportation. We figured this out when the teachers began to discuss where they lived. New York City is laid out logically in a grid, and twenty city blocks equal a mile. My new job would be two miles from Cornell University Medical School, where we lived in student housing. It might as well have been in another country. It was easy to get there, but it was a world away for a relatively sheltered young woman. I had thought I wanted to try working with older children, and there was an opening in third grade. There were seven third grade classes, and

I was assigned a group called "Three-Seven", the lowest IQ group. It took all my energy to keep them sitting in their chairs.

The floors were green and gray Kentile blocks, so each child stood on a grey block when they lined up. It was a job to keep them in their seats and interest them in anything, but I succeeded in teaching them second-grade level work and getting them to stand in line when we had to go to the lavatories. This was progress. In December of that year, a first-grade teacher retired, and I begged the principal to give me that class. He did what I asked, and my third grade had twelve teachers before the end of the year. No one could handle them. For the next few years, I kept my excellent first-grade classes and was assigned several student teachers from Hunter College. I eventually left to have my first child, Kim,

When Eddie graduated from medical school in 1965, we moved to Virginia with our new baby girl. I worked as a sub for a while when a fellow teacher told me about a part-time job teaching in WIN's Welfare Incentive Program. The students were women who were about my age. They were in the welfare system and were motivated to get out. The program provided them with on-the-job training and classes leading to the high school equivalency exam. I taught the English section of the GED class. The rooms we used were places where they could have on-the-job training. At the Veteran's Administration Hospital, I encountered some unsettling experiences before arriving at my classroom. The smell of urine and mashed potatoes greeted me at the door, and I had to walk past young paraplegic men lying on their stomachs and racing their ambulatory beds through the corridors. They were only about eighteen years old. Another young patient had tried to commit suicide by putting a gun in his mouth. He did not die but lost a portion of the front of his face. He wore a surgical mask, and he pulled it down to show me his face whenever he saw me. He did this to medical students, and the shock was intense. Eventually, you can get used to anything. I saw him at least fifty times.

One evening, driving faster than I should, I got my second speeding ticket in Richmond. Enjoying having the top down on my husband's MG Sprite. My hair was long, and it was blowing behind me. I was only doing 45, but it was a 35 MPH speed limit. The siren went off behind me, and I pulled over. The young policeman wrote me a ticket and then asked me to get out of the car. I was largely pregnant, which he hadn't seen before I stood up. He had to help me out of this tiny, low car. He turned red, and I think he wanted to undo the ticket. He kept apologizing. I told him that I had just seen my husband, a resident at the Medical College of Virginia, who was going to Vietnam very soon.

Later that evening, the same policeman rang my bell and asked me to return the ticket, as he had given me the wrong part. He was a perfect gentleman. I said, "Please come in while I get it." He replied, "I am on duty; I will wait out here." I gave him the ticket, and he left.

Since I had a prior ticket, I knew my license would be suspended for two months. I was running out of time. I needed my job. My baby was due in three months, and I needed my license back as soon as he was born. Residents sleep at the hospital every other night and on weekends, so I had to depend on myself to get a sick baby or five-year-old to a doctor. I went down to the Motor Vehicle Bureau to hand in my license for the sixty days. They took it and looked at my record. There was no sign of the ticket under discussion. Of course, because I told them about the ticket, they suspended my license anyway. I now had to take the bus to work, and in 1969, in Richmond, the buses were segregated. I was appalled at how black people had to sit in the back of the bus. None of my adult students had ever complained to me about this, and when I told them how I felt, they said they were sorry I had to see it. I had no plans to come back to the south after that.

The happy ending to my teaching in Richmond came when the LPN in a starched white uniform and cap brought me my new baby boy. As she entered the room, she said, "I told the other nurses that this was MY baby to deliver." Ida Mae had been one of my students in the WIN Program. We had tears in our eyes. It was a proud moment for both of us.

CHAPTER 27

1961–1965 · Cornell University Medical School, New York City

The medical students in the first year lived on the third floor of Olin Hall. Starting at the staircase, the students were assigned rooms by alphabetical order: Geiger, Hardy, Kappler, Kayser, Meyer.

Jack came from the Midwest and had graduated from Grinnell, where he was all known for his baseball prowess. His father had a Miller High Life beer distributorship in Davenport, Iowa. There was no Miller Lite then, or they would have been wealthy. When Jack's father died, his brother-in-law took over running the company for his mother. Each summer, Jack drove a Miller truck for ten years through high school, college, and medical school to deliver beer to taverns. Jack said, "I liked the physical labor and access to the beer. I also made a little money playing semi-professional baseball, putting my fastball to use. My mother lived alone, so she was happy that I spent the summers with her. She was a wonderfully sweet and beautiful woman." At one time, he shared with us that his mother had warned him to gargle with antiseptic when he came home from going to bars in New York.

Jack began to date Mary Jean, who had come to New York from Scotland. Mary Jean, Phyllis, and Maureen were roommates who worked as airline stewardesses and had too much time on their hands. They liked practical jokes and were at Olin Hall so often that Aaron, the night watchman, let them in with no questions. Late one afternoon, knowing that the guys didn't lock their doors, they slipped in quietly and found his roommate, Ron, studying, and Jack was out. They asked Geiger to step out for a minute and proceeded to put all of Jack's underwear into a laundry bag and steal all of Geiger's condoms. When Ron finally figured out what was going on, he chased them to the elevator to no avail. They put the underwear in a locker in the East Side terminal and then left clever clues about how to find it.

Jack tried for two days to figure out the clues, but he finally forced Mary Jean to tell him where the stuff was, and she gave him the key. He had to take a bus there, and when he put sufficient funds in the slot and pulled out the loose underwear, one of the large doors opened. Hundreds of arriving passengers caught Jack gathering up his underwear and Geiger's condoms. He returned Geiger's condoms, which were very expensive.

Ed was engaged to Mary, and they were planning a wedding for the following summer. He had also gone to Cornell, but Gus had not known him. They became friends quickly. Once they married and Mary moved to New York, we also became good friends. For my own wedding, Mary lent me her crinoline to wear under my wedding dress. Her mom sent it from Chicago. Mary and Ed were not at our wedding because they had the opportunity to travel to Mexico at Cornell's expense, with Dr. Lenahan to research a disease transmitted by birds. After they got there, Mary got me a job with the physician, whom I had not met, typing his research papers. He sent them to his secretary at Cornell Medical School, and I used that office to do the work. Remember that I was a first-grade teacher. On one of the reports, I added a little note to the Dr. Lenahan, "Can you write more slowly? Your handwriting is very bad."

He wrote back to me, "Your typing leaves a good deal to be desired as well." I cannot believe I did that, nor that he didn't fire me. My husband was a medical student. Who was I to criticize a faculty member?

One afternoon that we all remember, Jack was on York Avenue, and Ed was in an open window across the street. "Hey Meyer, throw that ball up here," he yelled. There was an older man, probably drunk, on the sidewalk, and he kept encouraging Jack to see if he could do just that.

Jack wound up and threw the ball RIGHT INTO THE WINDOW. The man went crazy, yelling, "Did you see that kid? The kid threw the ball right into the window. Did you see that kid?"

George was the most sophisticated of us all. His mother had instilled a great love of the arts.

He and Jack saw a sign on a passing bus advertising Peter Pan, played by Mary Martin. At that time, she was one of the hottest Broadway stars during the depression. She had starred in South Pacific, *The Sound of Music* and was famous for *My Heart Belongs to Daddy.*

George was thrilled, "Look! Mary Martin is playing Peter Pan!"

Midwest Jack asked, "Who is Mary Martin?" George was astonished and suddenly realized that even though these young people were at the top of their classes all over the country, many of them might not know about theater, opera, and museums, as had been his privilege. Every Sunday, George slept late, and we woke him up and went to the Hospital of Special Surgery for lunch, where they served a wonderful meal of fried chicken and mashed potatoes with gravy.

I keep saying "we." I did not attend classes, but I was in the group at the medical school. When they were freshmen, I was still in college in Baltimore, but I visited often. Gus had a cot under his bed, and he would put it up and sleep in Ron's room, sharing the bathroom with me. Today, everyone sleeps together, so the story sounds like a lie, but I have guys who will swear to it.

When they were sophomores, I taught on Long Island, planning our wedding and living at home. I drove into the city almost every weekend and brought things like Lasagna cooked for us by two brothers who owned the deli, where we often bought sandwiches. Sandwiches are incredible when made in New York City Delis.

Jack and Ron both came to my prom weekend at the College of Notre Dame of Maryland. I fixed them up with Lorette and Kathy, and they had a fantastic time. The day after the prom, we went to the reservoir. We swam and ran around like children; Kathy and Lorette had brought fake guns and colored cowboy hankies to wear as masks. These future teachers and doctors ran around, saying, "Stick em up. this is the Big H." (The big holdup)

This seems strange in the retelling. It is one of those things … you had to be there.

Recently, Jack gave me the best compliment. "We all looked forward to the weekends you visited."

These are unforgettable memories for me. Gus (who is still Eddie to me) and I married before the third and fourth years and lived in the same building as Mary and Ed.

We ran to the roof together, having heard an explosion during the Bay of Pigs' week because we thought it was a war; we went to the Saint Patrick's Day Parades together. We sat in our apartment and cried together on the weekend of John Kennedy's death. We had the first baby, Kim, who attended graduation. Kim is in her fifties. We are all eighty. We treasure our memories and friendships.

CHAPTER 28:

1962 · What Did He Do With the Toilet Paper?

In medical school, Ron moved into the room with Gus in Olin Hall when Ed moved out to get married. During the summer, when there were no med school classes, we lived on Long Island, about 50 miles from New York City, and Ron lived on Greenwood Lake in New Jersey. Ron always had a lovely date, and on an unusual day off, we went home with Ron to New Jersey. His parents were warm and welcoming. They lived in a large, lovely home. Ron's mom invited us to come out the night before and promised she would have a cookout for us.

 The family kept a boat on the lake, and the four of us planned a ski day. The water was tranquil, and the sun was hot above our heads.

Barbara, Ron's date, was a nurse. She and I shared a room, and his 14-year-old brother shared his bathroom with us. Remember that I only had sisters and attended a Catholic women's college. After a few runs, we stopped for a snack; Ron let the boat drift and said, "I am sorry that you have to share that bathroom. At 14, my brother is not good at cleaning up after himself." "Yes, I blurted out. Your brother doesn't brush his teeth or flush the toilet. I don't know what he is doing with his toilet paper. He pees and leaves the urine there."

 Everyone was staring at me. For a minute, there was a stunned silence and then a roaring laugh from the guys. That is how I learned, at age 22, that boys did not wipe, just shook.

CHAPTER 29

1965 · The Tart at the Wedding

Virginia was to be our home for five years at least. We were thrilled to be invited to a party at the home of Audrey Reynolds McGuire and Hunter McGuire. Hunter was an attending in surgery at the Medical College of Virginia and the great-grandson of another Hunter McGuire, personal doctor to Stonewall Jackson during the Civil War.

A sprawling house with several porches sat on top of the hill looking over the lake in the back of the McGuire's beautiful, brick home, which had been in the family for years. This was a party for the interns and residents in the surgery department. While we were sitting there looking out at this beautiful lake, one of the other women who had been there for a while described Hunter and Audrey's wedding. At the top of the hill, twenty hay bales with white satin cushions were scattered around for seating. The ceremony was held on the hill above the sparkling lake and green lawn. With the trays of great *hors d'oeuvres* being served, the cocktail hour was lovely on a cool, sunny day. With the help of men dressed in white jackets, everyone boarded the catamarans, where a cold champagne dinner had already been laid out. Gold Chiavari chairs were arranged for ten people per boat. A separate catamaran carried the band, which circled the lake. The menu was cool, cold lobster and sliced tenderloin with crunchy green beans. Lemon Chess tarts and Pecan tarts were served with coffee and tea. The wedding cake was waiting on the hill as the guests disembarked. Coffee and tea were available in giant silver urns and the most delicate of china cups.

These were the FFV, standing for the First Families of Virginia.

Hunter Maguire and his wife invited the interns and their wives, and we were more than honored. I was feeling strange and out of place, knowing not one person. Trying to make conversation, I said to an elderly southern lady next to me, "These pecan tarts are delicious." Of course, my New York accent gave me away. "Sweetheart," she said. "You are in the south now, and a pee can is what you keep under the bed. This is a puh-con."

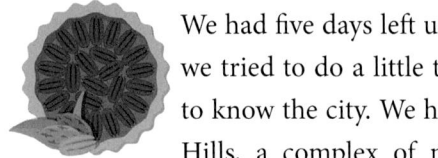 We had five days left until the internship again, and we tried to do a little touring in Richmond and get to know the city. We had an apartment in Westover Hills, a complex of modern apartments running along a creek. Each apartment had a balcony, so we spent time sitting outside with Kim in a playpen. Across the creek was a huge swimming pool, and we made a few friends before the internship began.

I was about to begin the five most difficult years of my life, with a year in Vietnam to follow.

It was a good thing I didn't know it.

CHAPTER 30

1965 · Sleep Where?

Kim was born in 1965, just in time to attend Cornell's Medical School Graduation. I made two beautiful matching dresses for us. We had a small party in our tiny apartment and went to Long Island to spend a few weeks with Grandpa and Grandma Kappler in Lake Ronkonkoma. In June, we moved to Virginia to a lovely two-bedroom apartment with a pool, and in July, Dr. Kappler began his surgical training at the Medical College of Virginia internship. He had a black old-fashioned doctor's bag that Eli Lilly gave to all graduating medical students, engraved with their names followed by the initials M.D.

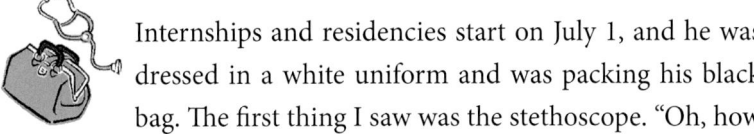 Internships and residencies start on July 1, and he was dressed in a white uniform and was packing his black bag. The first thing I saw was the stethoscope. "Oh, how exciting, Doctor. Let me see what else you have in there." I investigated the bag and saw a toilet kit and clean underwear. "I'm going to sleep at the hospital," he said quietly.

"Oh, no, you are not! I have never stayed alone in my life—and now with a new baby in a city where I don't know even one person. What are you thinking?"

How had I not known? In New York City at Cornell, where we had been, the residents slept at home and ran across the street when called. We had been swamped getting the right internship, having our first child, and running out to Long Island to paint our used furniture for our Richmond apartment. Somehow, the fact that he would sleep at the hospital every other night and weekend was a surprise. Thus began the formation of my mother-daughter relationship.

Her daddy was gone most of the time, and this tiny child became my roommate with equal rights. If I stayed up late, so did she. If I slept late, so did she.

I took her to the playground in our apartment complex and found a few friends for each of us. This way of life lasted five years until our son and her new baby brother, Christopher, was born. Six months later, the surgical residency ended, and my husband shipped out to Vietnam for a year.

CHAPTER 31

1969 · Am I Robin or Am I Sally?

Prominent women members of the Woman's Auxiliary to the AMA approached me. I had started a group called the Surgery Wives Club, which flourished. They wanted to establish a chapter of the Woman's Auxiliary to the Student American Medical Association (WA-SAMA). They invited several women for lunch and included the wives of medical students, interns, and residents. It is impressive how intuitive these women were and they formed a slate of officers that worked very well together.

We named our local chapter after Captain Sally Louisa Tompkins, a Confederate nurse, and the only woman to be commissioned into the Confederate Army. This led to people calling us Sally at conferences, since the name of the chapter was listed above our own names on our name tags.

Our local chapter was very successful, and during my third year, I was voted president-elect on the national level. Members were spouses of medical students, interns, and residents interested in making health care changes. I had a budget for travel, and I and I had a plan on how to use it. My husband was going to Vietnam, and I knew that it was going to be a long year.

CHAPTER 32

1970 · Uncomfortable Is an Understatement

"This baby is three weeks late," I complained to the walls. "I feel like a Thanksgiving Day parade balloon, ready for the music and the parade to begin, worried that I might blow up any minute." I am 5'6" with long brown hair, a first-grade teacher, and a mom. I usually weigh 117 pounds. Today I weigh 143. My suitcase is packed for the hospital with a box of Yodels hidden inside. I had not had chocolate for nine months, and I dreamed of eating them as soon as the baby was born. I waddled to the front door to look out at the snow.

"What are you waiting for?" I asked the baby. "We all want to meet you," I whined, just as my five-year-old daughter, Kim, came running into the room. "Who are you talking to? "Our baby, I am inviting him to get out here to play with you."

"Mommy. It is snowing! Can we go outside and build a snowman?"

The last thing I wanted to do was go out into the cold and get down on my knees in the snow, but she had been cooped up all day, so I agreed.

"Get your ski outfit on; you need a hat and mittens. I will get some bowls and things to dig with."

"Thank you," she said, "thank you. You are the best mommy in the whole world."

I put on my husband's spring skiing wind pants and tied them with a long ribbon around my chest above the baby bump. We didn't have a name for it in 1970.

Kim and I looked through the fridge for some things to fashion a face. We found a significant carrot for his nose, a raisins package for his smile, but nothing for the eyes.

"I can get two black checkers from my game!" Kim said, running from the room. I found gloves and my husband's ski jacket, and out we went.

It was unusual to have enough snow in Richmond, Virginia, to build a snowman. We had to take advantage of this. I never have the right tools for a job, but I had brought out some pots with handles. We used these to gather enough snow for the bottom of our snowman.

When it was large enough to satisfy us, we packed it until it was sturdy enough to stand alone and began to make the rest of the snowman. This was not as easy. "I think we have to roll it and pack it until it is hard enough to stay in place," I told Kim. We began rolling a giant snowball until it was big enough to form a top for our little man. How will we get it up there? I was a city girl and had never built a snowman in Brooklyn. Snowmen were Daddy's job, but Daddy was a surgery resident and rarely home.

"Let's think about this and make a plan," I said, "but let's make snow angels first." I just wanted to lie down for a minute, my back was aching, and the baby was restless. While we were making snow angels, Kim had a brilliant idea. "Let's get a towel, roll the big ball onto it, and lift it on top." She was off and running, leaving a snow trail on the dark green carpet.

Kim announced, "Before you say anything, I know this is a good towel, but it was the one could reach. Okay?

 "Get up, and we will put it on," she ordered me. I rolled my huge body over until I could get a knee out from under me and crawled to the fence to pull myself up. "Mommy, you are funny and look like a bear in Daddy's coat." "GRRRRRI," I croaked, and under my breath, I said, "What in heaven's name does a bear sound like?"

We rolled the snowball onto the towel and lifted it on top and thank God it stayed. "I have an idea," said Kim. "You are always telling me that a girl can be anything. Why can't it be a snow girl? We can make a skirt for her and get a pretty hat."

"Go into the kitchen and get my red apron with the ruffles on the front of it," I told her. It had not been worn in quite a while. It was clean because I was NOT going to put a ruffled apron on this enormous body. We dressed our creation, gave her a face, and put my Easter hat from last year on her head. I felt severe pain as I dragged myself to the front steps and pulled up on the railing. At first, I thought I had hurt my back, but another pain soon struck. I did not want to alarm my daughter, but I went right to the phone and called my friend, Jolene, to come and get Kim, and then I called Eddie to come and get me. Kim and I both had our bags packed.

An hour later, I was in the delivery room. My doctor told me that he would have to use high forceps because the baby was facing the ceiling instead of the floor, and every time I pushed him down, the pubic bone pushed him right back up. It is called LOP. I thought it meant lopsided. "Fine," I answered, "I don't care how you do it, get this gigantic baby out of me." I was so tired from the snow day that I fell asleep until another pang of pain woke me up. During my little nap, a group of 15 men and two women had filed in, lining the back wall of the white-tiled operating room, facing the delivery table and ME! I thought I was in the swimming pool under the water with Dustin Hoffman, hiding from Mrs. Robinson. "Robin, I will use high forceps to turn the baby," my doctor said. "I want these medical students and residents to see how it should be done."

 "What is he thinking? He knows how extremely private and modest I am. OH MY GOD," I thought; they are real, and I know them! They were interns and residents with my husband, a chief resident. I just closed my eyes so I wouldn't have to make eye contact. After all, I had been physically uncomfortable all day; why not another half hour of mortifying discomfort?

The doctor sat this gigantic baby on my stomach in about 15 minutes. "You have a great big baby boy," he said as I began to cry. He weighed in at nine pounds and five ounces. Eddie would be going to Vietnam as a surgeon in a few months, and I had wanted this child before he left.

The orders were for one full year. When he came home, he would have two children to run to greet him…and one skinny wife.

CHAPTER 33

1970 · Leaving on a Jet Plane

John Denver sings, *"I'm leaving on a jet plane, don't know when I'll be back again,"* No matter where we are, my adult daughter and I will catch each other's eye, sharing a feeling that no one else around us understands.

I was thirty and Kim was five when my husband, her Daddy, left for Vietnam on September 6, 1970. The skies over Texas were clear and blue, a good day for flying. One airline painted their airplanes in rainbow colors, advertising "The end of the plain plane." No matter what color the plane was, it was taking her Daddy very far away.

Thirty years of growing up had not prepared me for this moment. Six weeks at Fort Sam Houston had not prepared my husband for this moment. I tried to commit to memory the appearance of this young, slim, blonde, blue-eyed soldier with creased khakis and a duffel bag, smiling as he got into the car. As a newly trained general surgeon, he was looking forward to an adventure. As the untrained mother of a six-month-old son and a five-year-old daughter, I was terrified, but I thought I was smiling bravely. Forty years later, my husband will tell you that he will never forget the look on my face as he and his friend, Ben, pulled out of the driveway.

CHAPTER 34

1970 · Communication Across the Nation

We had been staying with Helen and Ben in Texas. I decided to leave an hour after my husband left, and I summoned my courage to let go of the safety net provided by my friend, Helen, and her one-year-old daughter, Whitney.

On our own, I explained to my daughter, Kim, that she would be the navigator, and I would tell her what highway we should be on, and she would read the signs. So, with my daughter in the front seat and my son in the back in a baby bed with two legs on the floor and no other means of holding it, I set out from Dallas for Little Rock, Arkansas.

"I can do this! I can!" I made it three miles and pulled into a shopping center, pretending to check the map. I gave in to the fear and sobbed my heart out. This man, who had been my high school boyfriend, my prom date, and my best friend, was leaving me, and I did not know when that jet plane would bring him back again or if I would even ever see him again.

We had explained about the Army and the hierarchy to Kim when Daddy got his orders. She saw me crying and said, "Mommy, I hate those damn generals."

"Me too," I said and put the car into gear to continue our journey.

I had been planning this trip for months as the National President of WA-SAMA, and my strategy was two-fold strategy: establishing relationships with as many of the chapters as I could and keeping myself busy for a year. I defined my theme as, "Communication Across the Nation", and I promised to visit any chapter in the United States, if they would organize a home for me to stay with my two children. I kicked off this campaign by driving a few hundred miles, visiting medical schools between Texas and New York.

I was a cheerleader in high school and college. I was bringing my ability to excite people to the individual groups across the country, setting goals together with these young women who were raising families and supporting men studying to be physicians.

Together with the chapter presidents, we would make plans and set goals that would work in their environment. The March of Dimes had invited us to work on programs for children's health, and the American Medical Association was counting on us to encourage health professions. Our local hospitals were grateful for any fundraising we accomplished. So, I carried the banner for our goals and inspired all the young women I met.

There were WA-SAMA chapters at almost every medical school in the country, and I visited as many of them as I could. We set up plans for each of the areas.

Each chapter had its own goals, and I had mine: to hold the branches together and see the good things these young women could accomplish for medicine. I wanted to make them aware that their lives might sometimes be complicated married to physicians and of what they could do for the medical profession. We accomplished raising the awareness of all the existing medical professions where careers were fulfilling.

We held a national convention yearly, and mine was in St. Louis, where I was a guest speaker at the American Medica Association convention. The beautiful hotel impressed me. I was given a two-bedroom suite and invited my fellow officers to stay with me.

For the next thirty days as we travelled, we stayed with young members of WA-SAMA. The interim trip was good for me. The host family husbands were fabulous, washing my car, filling it with gas, playing with my children, and even babysitting while their wives and I were attending the meetings where I was an honored guest. They saw that their wives could be in my position, alone for a year with two children, and they wanted to help me. I had mapped out a trip that would commit me to three hours of driving daily, with a few free days. I had a small budget and I paid, with my own money, for everything it did not cover.

I was honored in many of these cities. In Little Rock, I called in the hogs, chanting. "Suey, Suey Suey." The governor presented me with the keys to the city. We put many plans into action at these individual chapters. One new friend took us to the Polly Flinders factory outlet in Cleveland, and I bought Kim her kindergarten wardrobe. Polly was a high-end designer for children's clothing. I would not have purchased them retail.

CHAPTER 35

1970–71 · Travels With Kim

It took us one month to drive to Long Island, where my family lived. I rented a house around the corner from my father and sister. I needed a support group, adults for me, and cousins for Kim, who attended the school where I had my first teaching job. On the first day of school, the teacher asked the children to introduce themselves and say something about their summer.

When it became Kim's turn, she stood and said, "I am Kimi Kappler, and this is my Polly Flinders dress." I had indoctrinated her because I was so excited to buy wholesale.

I was happy to be living near my sisters and their little ones. I had a few opportunities to teach at the high school. My first-grade students were now Sophomores, and I had many of them in class. They all remembered me and were as happy to see me as I was to see them.

Kim rode the school bus with her cousin, Michael, who was in first grade. One day she got off the bus in tears and was inconsolable. When she could gather herself to talk, she said that one girl told everyone she had no father. "I do have a daddy, don't I?" "Of course, you do, sweetheart. Let's go inside and look at all our pictures together." I had not realized how hard this was for her. The next day, she armed herself with a picture Eddie had sent in his uniform surrounded by the jungle. I continued to travel for WA-SAMA and used my teaching dollars to pay the expense of bringing my children with me. Planes were not as crowded then, and I often got three seats across. Kim would sit by the window, and we would put Christopher in between us, lay him on the middle seat, and put the seat belt around his little body. He was such a good baby, and she was such a grown-up big sister that travel was easy. When we arrived at the airport, I would get a wheelchair, put Kim into it, and Chris on her lap. Diaper bags were my carry-ons, and I would hang them on the wheelchair handles. WA-SAMA members would meet me at the airports and host us in their homes. Those who had children, were happy to have us. We stayed with many people we had never met and were never guests for more than three days.

CHAPTER 36

1971 · Hong Kong Harbor

We met Daddy in Hong Kong that year and went to Bangkok for what the Army called R&R, rest and relaxation from a war zone. I didn't take Chris because, at sixteen months, he did not have all his shots, and I was afraid he would get sick traveling in the Far East. He stayed home, but that is another story. Kim was a great traveler. Our first stop was in California, where we stayed with friends. Joan took us to Hollywood and Universal Studios and finally to the airport, sending us off to Japan. We stopped for two days in Tokyo. We went to the commissary to buy gifts, and I bought a kimono robe for myself. Kim chose a kimono, a sash, and a parasol. I began packing the items to be sent to the States. "What are you doing with my new clothes?" Kim asked suspiciously. "I am sending them home." "Oh, not mine. I am going to wear them."

As we walked through the streets of Tokyo, Japanese people stopped us and asked us if they could take her picture.

 We traveled to Nikko by train to the park where the three monkeys are carved: Hear no evil, Speak no evil, and See no evil. In the United States, it is a popular way to pose three people for a photo.

"Let's go to Hong Kong a day early to wash our hair and rest until Daddy gets here tomorrow."

When we arrived at our hotel, we were hungry. There was an open-air restaurant in the lobby, and we sat there to order sandwiches. We were sipping our Cokes, talking about how lucky we were to get a flight the same day, when Kim jumped up from the table and ran toward a soldier in the lobby, calling out, "My daddy, my daddy, I haven't sawn you for a whole year." He picked her up, and a group of people formed around us. One woman said, "Aren't you jealous that she is getting all the attention?" I smiled at her, tears running down my face, "No, this year has been hard on her missing him," Then he hugged me and said," I knew you would be a day early."

 Landing in Hong Kong in 1970 was an experience never to be forgotten. Etched in my memory, it resembled a picture from a middle school geography class workbook. Visible all along the river were hundreds of brown boats called junks. These operated as a city. Tied together for miles, each junk had a sign telling what it was. Our guide pointed out the pharmacy. The next in line was the doctor's office and then the hospital.

The boats were loosely tied together so you could walk across from boat to boat along the water's edge. There were tiny bridges between boats, and some people had small vessels they used to travel between the ships.

The junk is shaped like a colossal pineapple, cut in half and scooped out. It has metal-type roofing to protect from the sun, and the people use the surrounding water for everything, drinking water, washing, cooking, and eliminating waste. Nothing is sanitary.

On our first night, the concierge from the hotel suggested we have dinner in Aberdeen. Aberdeen is known for its floating restaurant, the size of a cruise ship, sparkling with colored lights reflected on the water. It looks like a magnificent pagoda.

 The taxi dropped us at a dock near the restaurant, reassuring us that he had notified the maître d', and their water-taxi was coming to pick us up.

Americans don't realize that when traveling, our clothing and shoes give us away immediately. Eddie was wearing khaki pants and a button-down shirt with a blue blazer. We were uncomfortable when a rat pack of children surrounded him, hugging his legs and running their hands up and down his body, saying, "Hey GI, give money." We were stranded on the dock waiting for the small boat to pick us up for the restaurant. When it pulled up, the driver said something in Chinese, and the children jumped back into their motorboat and left quickly, searching for more GIs.

Having had a delicious dinner in this beautiful restaurant with Chinese lanterns reflecting in the water, I felt guilty for being so lucky, well-fed, and healthy. I wish I could have done something for those children.

THE RICKSHAW with a driver.

 We thought we would like to walk through a downtown area when we saw a Rickshaw and a river. Kim wanted to ride in it, so we hailed the driver, decided on a price and Kim climbed in. We would

walk beside them. Obviously, the driver did not understand that. He took off running. In all the traffic it was hard for us to keep an eye on the Rickshaw. We were running after it as fast as we could, and Kim was turned around looking at us. Finally, she screamed at the driver. "STOP! STOP!" and he did. We caught up and Eddie lifted her out of the Rickshaw and the driver left.

"What happened?" Kim asked when she stopped crying. I said, "We're not sure." And this brave little five-year-old replied in a shaky voice, "I will never forget this!"

BANGKOK

Bangkok was our next stop after Hong Kong. Bangkok is a beautiful city, but it seemed that many people there were very poor.

 We hired a driver for three days, and he showed us the city with its parks and famous Buddha. Our driver suggested, "We should go to Pattaya Beach and spend one night." He made arrangements for an outing in the Bay of Siam. He was like a tour guide, saying to us, "You must go to the commissary nearby to buy food for lunch on the boat." We found what we needed and went on to the beach. The small ship was something out of a storybook and looked like the wooden boat with white sails that we had seen at Disneyland. It was docked in a private cove where the water was clear and clean. The crew was a father and son. They did not speak English, but the boy was six, and Kim was five. They became friends immediately, and he showed her how to jump off the boat's side into the cool water. They swam and jumped and laughed together. It was beautiful to see.

An exciting part of the day was unpacking lunch. Sharing our culture, we bought white bread, peanut butter, two kinds of jam, and a case of root beer to drink. They loved the food, and we gave it to them to take home.

Thailand is known as "The land of Smiles," and, with the cultural differences shared, we said goodbye, trying to show our feelings with giant smiles.

Two months after that trip, the year was over. My husband came home from Vietnam. We spent a few weeks visiting our families. Our next Army station was Colorado Springs, where Kim attended a school that faced Pike's Peak. We hiked and skied, enjoying the beauty of Colorado for a full year.

CHAPTER 37:

1971 · Panties in Her Purse

Kim was such a funny little girl. On one of our hikes, while crossing a stream, my husband, an undaunted tease, picked Kim up and dipped her bottom into the water. She cried and cried and demanded her other clothes, and I had brought a change of clothing for her but no underwear. We redressed her commando, and she kept saying, "Mommy, this feels awful. Why did you forget my panties?"

A few weeks into the school year, Kim asked me to walk her to school, and she got her books and her little purse that she had begun carrying everywhere.

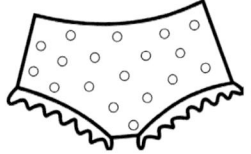 "I need company going to school," she said, "those mean girls are making fun of me, and I don't want to walk with them anymore." It took me a few minutes to discover that they made fun of her because she carried panties in her purse. Daddy had to rein in his teasing!

CHAPTER 38:

1970 · Aint Nobody

"Look at Robin," my sister Janet said. "She wants to be a teacher. Robin is the bossiest little girl on Third Street in Brooklyn." She lined up children on the bottom step of a twenty-step outdoor staircase of a brownstone house as we watched. As the teacher, she asked them questions, and if they gave the correct answer, they could move up a step. If they missed, another child had a chance to answer the same questions. No one else was ever allowed to call out the answer. After college, Janet and Robin were both teachers.

GREEN HANDS & SOBBING BOYS

The English and French majors passed us in the hall, smirking because we might be carrying ABC signs and children's books like "Wind in the Willows." They would not laugh when we had job offers immediately. Getting a teaching job in 1962 was only a matter of choosing a school district and applying. There was a desperate need for teachers at a salary of five thousand dollars a year. I chose a school five miles from my family's home, where I would live for the next year.

The twenty-five students in my first grade were a mixture. Many were children of scientists working at Brookhaven National

Laboratory. Add a few average middle-class children, a few naughty boys, and a few outstanding girls.

The principal was a young man who later became the Superintendent of Schools. He was the perfect principal for a beginning teacher. The faculty members were very young, and the teacher's room was a happy place. Later, when I worked as a substitute teacher, it became apparent to me that the leadership trickled down to the staff. Some schools had a tense and miserable attitude in the teacher's rooms. Eating lunch in the classroom was a choice in those schools where principals were uncompromising, and the staff was unhappy.

As the months went by, there were memorable experiences, and this class was no different. Arthur was very naughty. At six, they have not lived long enough to be called bad. Arthur was working at the easel in the back of the room. He painted both his hands until they looked like green gloves and began running around the room, terrorizing everyone. However, he never really touched anyone. I led him directly to the sink, kept him from getting the paint on me, and helped him wash his hands.

 Another day, three boys were acting out in class, and it was almost three o'clock. I told them that they had to stay after school. These were all bus children out on Long Island, and I planned to show what could happen when you misbehave and miss the bus. I took the rest of the students to the school bus parking lot, intending to rush back and escort the three who rode on the same bus. However, another teacher stopped me to talk in the parking lot, and I forgot the three musketeers inside. The buses left! Quickly, I rushed in with a terrible feeling of guilt. Walking to the principal's office with the three boys crying, I felt ridiculous. The principal was holding back laughter as I explained what I had done. "It is your mess; how do you think you can clean it up?" he asked.

"Well, I guess I could drive them home?"

He asked the secretary to call the parents and explain. One of the mothers smiled at me and said, "You sure did cause yourself a mess of trouble." Her son, David, was one of my favorite students. In 1962, you could touch the children, and I often squeezed their little faces gently. One day, when David arrived, I touched his face, and my hand slid off. "David," I said, "What is on your face?" This beautiful little African American boy smiled and said, "I'se gray, and my Momma shines me in the morning with Dixie Mae Peach Pomade."

In 1970, when the surgical residency ended, it was time to pay the Army back for giving us the extra years in between. He was sent to Vietnam, and I moved with my own two children back to my family home. I did not want to raise them alone, even for a year. I enrolled in the school district. I would live near my sisters, who tried to comfort me. They told me the schools were desperate for subs, and I could probably work as many days as I wanted to.

I worked often, and one day, I was asked to sub in high school music. It is well-known that high school kids love to torture subs, but they loved this class, so I brought in a small record player and several records and made my lesson plan around that.

 When I arrived and ran my eyes down the class lists, and I was delighted to see that David, now grown up, would be in the afternoon class. It had been nine years since I taught these children. David Kenney strolled into the room, a very cool kid acting very much in charge and said, "Hey, hey, Hey" to the other students. He sat down, and I called the roll. When I got to his name, I said, "I think I know you. Are you sometimes called "Bo"? This young man stared at me for a full minute, and the class was quiet, and then he smiled and said, "Ain't nobody to give THIS teacher a hard time today."

CHAPTER 39

1981 · The Great Gatsby Gang of Saratoga Springs

 A sleek, black limo pulled into the driveway of our small farm in Amsterdam, New York, promptly at 6:00 p.m. Dressed in gowns and tuxedos, we lifted our champagne flutes in a quick toast. Our group included our adult children and their dates. Our daughter, Kim, was home for the weekend, having just begun her first job in New York City. She brought her friend, Drew, who had been the basketball team captain at Cornell the previous year when they were seniors. Kim had not dated Drew as an undergraduate. Basketball and hockey were the same seasons, and she had dated the hockey team's captain. Kim had set a goal to date every team captain before graduation, so when she ran into Drew in New York City after college, she had unfinished team captain business, and they began to see each other. Our son, Christopher, 17, was headed to Syracuse University in the fall. His date, Alisha, had been his friend since they were toddlers.

We enjoyed several more sips of champagne in the limo on the way to the National Museum of Dance, 30 miles away in Saratoga Springs, where we were attending a celebration of dance.

The museum's long driveway, edged in a gorgeous splash of color, surrounds the circular flower garden. We were assisted out of the limousine by young men in white dinner jackets and entered the museum through the Grand Foyer. Our high heels tapped excitement on the gleaming marble floor, and the shimmering crystal chandeliers created soft lighting. "If you look at the ceiling, just below the carving, you can read the names of the celebrities who have been inducted into the Dance Museum," I told everyone. After accepting a sparkly flute of champagne from the silver trays, we were outside again in a vast tent festooned with pink tulle and white lights and displaying a life-sized ballerina floating on a trapeze above our heads. Upstate New York has cool evenings, and the temperature was perfect. The centerpieces on the table looked as if they had come from an English garden filled with ranunculus, hydrangeas, lavender, and lily of the valley interspersed with lush greens.

We headed to our table, set with pink floor-length table-cloths, gold flatware, white china, and sparkling crystal glass-ware. As I put down my silver Judith Lieber evening bag, I asked myself, "How did we become part of this elegance in Saratoga, mingling with the summer racing people?" I was thrilled with such a magical evening, feeling comfortable with our intimate group of friends, a dynamic, sophisticated combination of people. The orchestra began to play "New York," a particular song for us, and we joined the dancers. The colors of the beautiful dresses whirling to the music added to the ambiance of the perfect evening.

A vintage sports car was being auctioned, and my handsome husband gave our young son $100 to buy five chances. Chris thought that was too much money, so he only bought three chances. The number that won the car would have been his fourth ticket—what a disappointment to a 17-year-old who had just gotten his license.

Another special place for summer was High Goal Polo, played three times a week. Famous polo players came from Argentina, bringing magnificent polo ponies. Each polo team had three professional players, the fourth being the Padrone. The Padrone is usually a wealthy American who pays the bills. The players are mainly from Argentina. One player was married to Fergie's mother, and Fergie was married to Prince Andrew of Great Britain—rarified air in upstate New York.

Chris was 11 when we started our membership, and he loved to bring friends. Four years prior, we had been given a guest pass to a party at the polo field and enjoyed it so much that we joined immediately and began attending matches where everyone was dressed to kill in jacket and tie, even the young boys. Christopher emerged from the woods with his cousin Steven, also 11. They had removed their ties and were bringing them to me to hold. "Mom," said Chris, "before you say anything, that woman told us that we did not have to wear our ties today because it is so hot."

"I did," that woman replied, "you have lovely boys; please come and join us for a drink! My name is Natalie Buchman."

We had champagne at our table, quickly filled our flutes, and joined them. They had set up for a party with silver dishes, assorted hors d'oeuvres, and a large floral centerpiece. Natalie was wearing a beige designer dress with a hat to march. Round tables were provided in the tent for the members, who brought their floor-length tablecloths and delicacies. We decorated our table with an embroidered lace, linen cloth, and a silver champagne bucket. Chairs were scattered for the comfort of the attendees. We decided that in the future, we would bring flowers.

We lined the chairs up at the edge of the polo field during the match. Natalie and Lou were about 20 years older than us, a stunning couple dressed to the nines. Lou, who was primarily bald, had a comb-over not to be believed. It looked quite elegant, and he got away with it. One day, Christopher asked us, "What do you think Lou looks like in the morning?"

The men always wore light-colored jackets and pants and had an array of fantastic Gucci ties. Natalie introduced their friends, Charlie and Dale, who were about ten years younger than us. Charlie had the most incredible white shoes with epaulets on the arch where they tied.

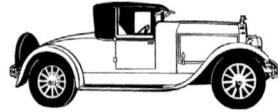 Kim was 16 that summer and looked quite beautiful. She wandered over to the table, and Dale and Charlie began conversing with her. Later she informed us that Charlie and Dale were lawyers who had a private investigative business. Irving and Elaine Kirsch arrived in their Jaguar, Nancy and Gary DiCresce in their Mercedes, and Susan and Tony DePaula in a vintage black Excaliber. Everyone was so friendly and immediately included our children. Later, Donna and Milton Seigal, old friends of Natalie's, joined our "gang." Milton was an orthodontist, and, like us, he parked his average car in another lot next to our jeep. The unique vehicles were a dramatic entrance to the polo field and tents. They had assigned parking spaces next to the tent, adding to the ambiance and finishing a perfect picture.

The tables were set up inside a white tent top, ready for guests who brought their varied tablecloths. Hats were *de riguer* for polo and added to the colorful dresses and jewelry; no matter the age the women looked beautiful.

We attended a Peter, Paul, and Mary concert with our children a few nights later and were leaving early to beat the traffic. Parked next to us was a white Corvette, and Kim was admiring it. Just then, a couple came towards it, and Kim said, "Oh, for heaven's sake, I thought I would see a cute guy who owned this car, and look, he has a girlfriend."

"Guess what," said the woman, "The car belongs to me. You don't need a boyfriend to have a car you like." I knew that I had seen her before, but I wasn't sure if she recognized me, and then she said, "I had a license plate with my name, Katie, on it, but guys were always calling me as I drove by, so I changed the plate." "Katie," I said, "I thought I recognized you. You helped us to choose our pool furniture last month."

"Yes, I recognized you as we were leaving polo last weekend. Are you members?"

"We are, and we love it. We have horses, we all ride, and Kim is on the horse-show circuit. Polo is great because we don't have to bring horses, and there is no pressure like there is at a horse show."

"Are you going to polo on Sunday?" Katie asked, and we said we would see each other there. I was delighted when I saw that Katie and John were part of Natalie's group, who had now embraced us.

We attended every black-tie party, sometimes as many as six during July and August. Natalie decided that we should support all the charity luncheons and would phone us before polo and say, "Today is a beautiful day. Wear hats and jewels." We all did as she suggested. In light summer dresses, the women walked on their tiptoes so that their high heels would not sink into the grassy polo area. Picnics became more elaborate as the summer went on, particularly for the Polo Picnic contest held in the middle of the polo season. We chose a Victorian theme for one of our group picnics, and our tables were surrounded by the classic cars that this group drove. Charlie and Dale had a Bentley with oriental carpet as the floor mats. Katie and John drove a white Excalibur, which reminded me of the *Chitty Chitty Bang Bang* car. Natalie and Lou had a Golden Shadow Rolls Royce complete with Grey Poupon's bottle in the glove compartment. People often pulled up next to them and asked, "Do you have any Grey Poupon?" Lou would pop out the jar and say, "But of course," mimicking the commercial.

The following year we went all out to win the prize for the best picnic. We decided upon a Hawaiian theme, and each of us contributed something unique. Katie and John's business, Imperial Pools, manufactured vinyl-lined swimming pools, so Katie brought a liner and spread it out at the edge of the field. It was 20 feet wide with a blue background. The men picked it up by the corners and set it on the grass like a fresh, top sheet on a bed. Katie also brought bags of sand to sprinkle at the edge. "Be careful not to get any sand on the grass; keep it all on the liner," Katie warned the young boys, one of whom was our son, Chris, who had brought his two best friends, Cullin and Eric. Cullin's parents manufactured small sailboats called Sunfish, and the boys brought two and set them up on the pool liner. The orange and purple Sunfish popped with the sun reflecting off the aqua liner.

Charlie, who had been social chairman of his fraternity, put dry ice in a bowl and made a smoking punch. Natalie ordered a roasted pig with an apple in its mouth, and I made a cake that looked like a palm tree. We all dressed in floral fabrics and grass skirts. The men wore colorful Hawaiian shirts. Christopher, Cullen, whose parents lent us the Sunfish, and Eric, a very handsome Puerto Rican boy, wore colorful Hawaiian shorts with white t-shirts. Polo began at 5:00 p.m., and we arrived at 2:30 p.m. to be ready.

Fifteen other families decorated equally impressive picnics; one couple had a white wooden gazebo around which they placed wicker, upholstered furniture. Fran Ingraham, Society Column Editor for *The Albany Times Union*, drove Mary Lou Whitney, the Grand Dame of Saratoga, in a golf cart. These prominent ladies judged the picnics. They stopped and spoke to the guests. Mary Lou Whitney asked if she could stand on the Sunfish. Eric jumped on with her to help her keep her balance. Photographers were everywhere, and the photo appeared in the paper and on the TV news that evening. Eric was thrilled.

Of course, we won the contest, and as we were cleaning up, the teenage boys took the dried ice into the woods. They wanted to experiment to see what would happen if they urinated on it. Just as they got it smoking and were mid-stream, Natalie walked by and saw them, and Eric said, "Uh oh, uh oh." Natalie retorted, "Don't think about it for a minute; if I had a Dinkus, I would join you."

Natalie and Lou were unique. Their business was importing feathers from China; she had learned to speak Chinese and was fluent in French. They had factories in Cohoes, New York, near Albany. During the Korean War, the government gave them the contract for the famous down jackets our soldiers wore. When the Korean crisis ended, they were given the machinery the government had supplied. With this equipment, they began to manufacture feather-down pillows and comforters. By the time we met them, they had sold the factory for $59 million, which they had shared with Lou's brother, who was his partner.

As a physician working with his hands, my husband wondered if we could keep up with them financially, but we never attended anything too expensive for us to join them. We looked forward to the Ballet Gala, a New York City Ballet fundraiser held in the Hall of Springs at Saratoga Performing Arts Center. The state park at Saratoga has several Romanesque buildings constructed by the Works Progress Administration when FDR instituted these projects to help people find jobs following the Depression. They have marble floors, beautiful columns, and the availability of curative waters.

Many years later, when bathhouses were out of fashion, the buildings began to be used for other purposes. One became the National Museum of Dance supported by Mary Lou with her wish to bring dance history to Saratoga. Many fundraisers opted to use these buildings for events.

One party was held at the Great Escape, an amusement park in Lake George. We enjoyed riding the Ferris wheel, the carousel, and playing the carnival games in black tie and gorgeous gowns. At the last minute, I had to change escorts. Emergency surgery on one of Eddie's patients prevented his attending. I had a secret date. Chris had his tux, he was 17, and I had recently gotten a red Corvette. I said, "If you go with me, you can drive us in the Corvette." Of course, he agreed, and this was the kind of party that would be fun for a teenager. The Great Escape wanted to publicize their newest ride, the Water Flume. We were given ponchos to wear over our clothing, and we loved it, screeching all the way.

At one point in the evening, there was an art auction. I was not looking for artwork, and I knew Chris would not be interested. We found all the games open and noticed a young woman trying to get the chicken into the pot. Chris walked over to her and said, "I can show you how to do this if you want me to." "Oh, yes, I have been trying, and I did not want to go to the art auction." "Neither did I, and my mom was willing to play games also." He began to show her how to hit the mallet and position the rubber chicken to fly across space to the pots. They were laughing together, and she finally got the hang of it. I was watching from the sidelines and laughing to myself. Chris had no idea he was teaching Maria Caligari, a principal dancer of the New York City Ballet. Later, he said, "She seemed so young and sweet." I explained that ballet dancers give up their teen years to live ballet. They go to the School of American Ballet at Lincoln Center and live in their dorms. They have private school classes. Dance is their life!

This was a memorable evening for both of us, and of course, Chris was comfortable with Natalie, Katie, and all the kids were crazy about Charlie. Maria Caligari introduced us to Jerome Robins! What an evening!

Our friends were often guests of honor. Irving and Elaine had given a great deal of money for the Suez Canal and were invited to a dinner in Tel Aviv, where they would be seated on the dais. Elaine informed us that wearing a dress with detail on the top is essential when you are on the dais. She bought a magnificent silver sequin gown and was very excited about the event and the trip until the day Israeli Prime Minister Menachem Begin's wife, Aziza, died unexpectedly. The dinner was canceled, and Elaine was devastated. However, she kept the dress and wore it to one of our parties. It was lovely with a dropped waistline and fantastic silver shoes. She planned to carry her Judith Lieber purse, which depicted the three monkeys: hear no evil, speak no evil, see no evil. The bag was made of Swarovski crystals.

The Irving and Elaine Kirsch Charitable Foundation now supplies money, goods, or services to the poor, rehabilitating alcoholics, drug abusers, and compulsive gamblers.

Katie and John were the guests of honor at a dinner held in a reinvented cave in Lyon, France, where they had established a pool business. They did not know they were the guests of honor. They got lost and were late for the dinner but made it in time for the speeches. In a lavender strapless dress, Katie's beautiful long, red hair was decorative enough for the dais. Katie also had a Judith Lieber crystal bag designed in the shape of three library books with a corded golden tassel.

Nancy and Gary were honored by Mutual of New York. Gary was named Man of the Year, and they were given a marvelous party. They chose the venue, The Museum of Racing, in Saratoga. We were all photographed standing inside the starting gate, which had been retired from the Saratoga Racetrack, and also in the dioramas of the jockey's dressing room with the scales, silks, and saddles behind us.

Elaine chaired a fundraiser for disabled children called "Satin, Silks, and Stars," and we were all seated with her guests. I was delighted to sit with Susan Lucci, as I was a long-time fan. She was friendly and talkative, as was her handsome husband, who is her manager.

Together, we supported every disease known to man along with the arts. The Albany Symphony, the Philadelphia Orchestra, the New York City Ballet, Saratoga Hospital, and Albany Medical Center were galas we enjoyed.

Natalie, Lou, Irving, Elaine, Milton, and Nancy are gone now, but the legacy they left with the rest of us makes us smile.

Gatsby's friends were the idle rich, but nothing was idle about these people. At Irving's 90th birthday party, I mentioned that I was tired from the summer season and looking forward to a rest. "I don't want to rest," said Irv, "I want to live!"

CHAPTER 40

1984 · The Sidewalks of My Life

My first sidewalk was on Third Street in Park Slope, Brooklyn, in the 1940s.

I earned to walk, roller skate, and ride my bike later on this sidewalk. I wore my first high heels. I danced with abandon in my confirmation dress and have the 16 mm movie to prove it. On summer days, my father would often open the fire hydrant for the kids in the neighborhood who gathered in swimsuits and beach shoes to run delightedly through the cold water, which surged out and could knock small children over.

My small world was enclosed by Fourth Avenue to the South and Prospect Park to the North, from Grand Army Plaza to Twelfth Street. This domain included candy stores, ice cream parlors, barbershops with red-and-white striped poles, pizza parlors, trolley tracks, and overhead wires supplying the power. You could climb onto the soda fountain seat and drink egg cream.

Methodist Hospital is still on Sixth Street, as are Saint Saviour's School and Church. In my blue pleated uniform and white starched blouse, I put in hundreds of miles back and forth to school and church. As I got older, I loved the freedom to go to all these places alone. Of course, I was never alone for long as I would "call for" friends to join me.

The corner of Fifth Street and Eighth Avenue was a "hangout" for the kids from Saint Saviour's. We met older friends who had gone on to different high schools after school. We met the cute boys from our class and the older ones who had gone on to Saint John's Prep, Xavier, Brooklyn Prep, and Brooklyn Tech.

Everyone in the neighborhood knew each other. My dad, who grew up on Third Street, was particularly plugged in. He received a telephone call from the garage around the corner one day. "Bring the girls over quickly; the Brooklyn Dodgers are here. Their car broke down." I met Pee Wee Reese, Gill Hodges, Roy Campanella, and Carl Furillo outside that garage. Pee Wee Reese gave me a nickel and told me to call him in ten years. The Dodgers were Brooklyn's heroes; meeting them was something special. You often met more than one as they lived near each other and traveled together by car. They did not make money earned by today's athletes, but they were beloved. Brooklyn went crazy with delight when the Dodgers won the World Series.

Manhattan was a subway ride away. We often went "into the city" for Easter Shows at the Roxy (Radio City Music Hall) or the Ringling Brothers Barnum and Bailey Circus in Madison Square Garden. In eighth grade, Jimmy Magee invited me to be his date for the spring formal at Xavier High School in Manhattan. My mom and her sister, Eileen, took me to Saks Fifth Avenue on the subway. I felt grown-up walking along "the sidewalks of New York" on Fifth Avenue. We came home with a pale green confection, which was the only time I wore it in Brooklyn.

We left Brooklyn six months later to move to our summer home in Lake Panamoka. The circumstances we left are not entirely known, but my sisters and I are researching. We have discovered this: My father has a dental laboratory and a partner so far. It was a considerable lab with many machines and probably $100,000 worth of equipment.

 One night I heard my parents whispering, and the partner's name came up often. The next day they told us we were moving. We recently discovered that the partner had embezzled the business, and Daddy lost everything. All his siblings lived near us. He would have had to have a powerful reason to leave. For the rest of my childhood, I considered Brooklyn my lost home. I can't say that I was unhappy during that time. High school in the 1950s was a fantastic experience.

When I was 18, I walked along the sidewalks of Baltimore, Maryland, to enter the College of Notre Dame. I appreciated the city, and I loved getting around on public transportation again. During student teaching in my senior year, I was assigned to an inner-city school with many sidewalks in the area leading to Baltimore's waterfront, which was then a dangerous place. As an art and sociology lesson for my first graders, I planned a giant bulletin board. I cut out identical paper doll-like figures from the light cardboard called Tagboard. The school was in the center, and each child colored in their features and clothing. I put in all the sidewalks in the neighborhood and had the children place themselves on the ones they used to walk to school. As the finale, I had one child pin an American flag on the school's roof. "Do you know," I asked, "what that is?" One little boy who lived on the docks excitedly blurted out, "It means we don't let Kat licks in here."

In 1963, I married Eddie, now a medical student. We lived in student housing on East Sixty-ninth Street and York Avenue. "Hooray, sidewalks again!" I was in for a surprise when I walked up the sidewalk on 69th Street to take the First Avenue bus to 116th street, P.S. 155, my assigned school. Originally an Italian neighborhood, the area was now called Spanish Harlem. I saw old Italian women carrying jugs on their heads on those sidewalks, refusing to leave their community or cultural ways. Across the street from the school was a garage. Occasionally, the garage door would go up to let long, black limos in or out. On an average school day, I took my first graders to the lavatory, and two men in trench coats and fedora hats exited from the boys' bathroom. I marched my class to the principal's office and reported grown men in the children's bathroom, demanding that he check it out. Later that week, the TV in my classroom went awry. I complained to the office, and the principal visited my classroom. "Mrs. Kappler," he warned, "stop asking about the strange things you see. The FBI is using our school as a base to investigate the mafia stronghold in the garage across the Street. You are calling attention to it."

My next sidewalks were in Richmond, Virginia, where my husband did his internship and residency. I walked our daughter in her new carriage and eventually taught her to ride a tricycle and roller-skate on that sidewalk. Later, I would push a small son in the same carriage on the same sidewalks. Eddie finished the surgery residency and entered the Army as he had promised. He was part of the Berry Plan, which deferred military service, and we sold that house with its sidewalks and spent the second year of military service in Colorado.

We chose upstate New York and a country home, and there again, no sidewalks. I spent the next 30 years raising children, keeping horses, and working for my community, which had very few sidewalks, but they were not significant during this stage of my life.

When our daughter was in college, she did an internship in Manhattan and lived at the 92nd Street Y. Her roommate was traveling, leaving an extra bed, and I jumped on a train to the city. It was a stormy day, and I could not get into the Y without Kim, so I walked all over the city until it was time to meet her. We had settled on Barbetta in the theatre district for dinner at 6:00 p.m. At 5:00 p.m., I went to the ladies' room at Macy's and repaired the damage the rain had done—I bought a new scarf to cover my dress's white neckline, which had absorbed all the soot in the city. My red Italian boots were damp, so I held them under the heated hand dryer. I fixed my makeup and took out my butane curling iron to do my hair. Hailing a taxi in front of Macy's, I gave the driver the address for Barbetta.

"It is a two-way street," he said," I can drop you across the street from the restaurant."

"Fine, just get me as close as you can so I don't get soaked. Thank you."

When he pulled up across from the restaurant, I noticed a divider in the middle of the street, and he said, "That side of the street is closed; you will have to go to the corner." "I will be okay; I can climb over it." I paid him and climbed onto the wooden barrier about two feet high. It was dark, and I took a leap of faith. Holding my umbrella above my head like Mary Poppins, I jumped off the orange barrier—into two feet of wet concrete! With the concrete sucking my boots like quicksand, I struggled to the sidewalk. The maître d' who must have been watching me from the window, opened the door and said, "Oh my, you need help! Stay right here." He brought me a chair and removed my boots as if I were royalty. "I will take these to the kitchen, and they will wash them off for you." He led me to the bar in my stockinged feet and gave me a glass of wine. When my daughter arrived and gave our name, he said, "Your mom is in the bar."

"Mom, you are only here for a day, and already you have had an adventure. Barriers and rope mean you are not supposed to go there." "I know, but I had to get to the sidewalk!" How could she possibly know what that sidewalk meant to me?

CHAPTER 41

1988 · Christopher Jon Kappler

Chris keeps his circle of friends small but is an entirely reliable friend when you are on his radar. When he was little, he was a delightful child. Chris did almost everything he was asked and always awoke with a smile. He never talked baby talk, and I doubt he has made a grammatical error in his life. When his friends came over to play, I often heard him correcting their grammar, but Chris was such a generous child that they allowed it. He is and was logical in his thinking. I quickly learned not to argue with him on a point he believed in because Chris would win on most subjects. He was a sensitive and loving child, smiling most of the time. He liked things like Lincoln Logs and science games. His favorite game was *1001 Things to Do with Electricity*. When Chris was five or six, he began taking apart unwanted toasters, electric mixers, telephones, and radios.

He showed a great deal of interest in robotics and computers. We enrolled him in summer courses for elementary school children held at Union College, and his love of computers began.

Looking back to a second-grade experience, Chris was tested for a gifted and talented program. He did not make the cutoff, but his teacher insisted that he belonged in the group and requested oral testing, and he was invited to join the group.

We were called in for a teacher conference in sixth grade, and Mrs. Dufresne explained that Chris was losing skills. His friend, Rebecca, copied his homework assignments from the blackboard and called him at night to remind him of things he had to bring to school for the next day. I spoke to Rebecca, and she said, "Mrs. Kappler, I have to do it for him; he cannot do it."

My husband had heard of Sylvan Learning Center from a TV ad, so we took him there to be tested. We thought perhaps he could not see the blackboard, but the eye exam proved otherwise. His IQ was so high I didn't know whether to kiss Chris or punish him. His grades were always middle of the road. We knew he was brilliant, but he couldn't seem to prove it.

The next step was a visit to a psychologist who told us we had to decide which was more important, the boy or the grades. We said, "The boy, of course." He spent two years at Sylvan, 30 miles away, and took computer lessons once a week with Joe. Eddie and I had dinner in a nearby diner while they worked.

Chris excelled in technology.

At the beginning of high school Junior year, he got a fabulous report card, and we thought we were home free. He had almost all As. A week later, his math teacher called me and said Chris was failing math. I promised to meet with him, and then I picked Chris up from school to take him to his SAT course at Union College. He got into the car, and I told him about the phone call from Mr. Rosemarino. Chris is very fair-skinned but turned ghostly white and asked me to pull over. I parked the car and looked at him as he said, "Mom, my report card was not real. I want to quit school, join the Army, and start over again."

"Oh my God, Chris, did you access the school's computer system?" He assured me that he had not, and the explanation floored me. He had gone to the Superintendent of Schools and said he was reporting on our school system's forms and needed some for his report. The Superintendent gave him all the documents, and he printed his report card. This precipitated another trip to the psychologist to admit that we were finally serious about the idea that the boy was more important than the grades. Teen suicides were in the newsweekly, and we were frightened. The psychologist made us face the fact that we had to understand that the three of us loved each other enough to do whatever it would take.

I had been in Carnegie Delicatessen a year before in New York City. With the tables' proximity, my friend and I began conversing with the two women next to us, who were visiting NYC. They were from Syracuse University, working on a program to test gifted and talented children with learning disabilities. As soon as I returned home, I called and was able to get an appointment at Syracuse. We spent two consecutive weekends, and Chris was tested. The result was "Gifted and Talented with Dyslexia."

I was working as a substitute teacher and removed myself from the list. I read to Chris every day after school. That year America was celebrating the 200th anniversary of the Constitution. I felt sure that the Social Studies Regents, a New York state exam for all schools, would be loaded with questions about the Constitution, so we concentrated on it. I was right, and he aced it.

We met with a committee of teachers who could grant students extra testing time for school and state exams. It took a great deal of dazzling them with data. I collected information from the

State Education Department to convince them that this could be done without certifying the child. They granted our request, but not without some weeping and gnashing of teeth.

English was the next hurdle. His teacher told me that 20 of the points would be spelling words. Chris spells phonetically, and he might automatically lose those points. With a great deal of study, he could spell a few of the words. He passed with a pleasant grade.

A big decision had to be made. Kim was at Cornell. We thought Chris would go there, but the guidance counselor recommended that we try to find a school just for him, not necessarily a family tradition.

My mind went back to Syracuse, where they had an untimed testing program and a contract between professor and student. The student could take all his tests on computers and would not receive any deductions for spelling. It looked like a perfect fit, so Chris wrote to the computer engineering department chairman and included a resume of what he had done. He told him we would be going to Cornell the following weekend to visit his sister, and we would be able to stop at Syracuse if he had time to meet with us.

The chairman called our house and told me this was a young man to be met. They clicked immediately, and the professor told Chris that if he came to Syracuse and maintained a 3.5 average, he would get his graduate degree tuition-free. He earned a Ph.D. in Computer Engineering in five years. He was named in the dean's list every semester and graduated with honors and awards.

Books were furnished through the Syracuse University Office for the Disabled, which got them from the Library of Congress program, Readings for the Blind.

He went through the Greek rush system and was invited to join ATO, the fraternity he liked best. After a year as a "brother,"

Chris decided that fraternity life was not for him. He had received the highest marks in the fraternity, being awarded a free year as a member. Hearing the brothers sort through the rushees was upsetting. He didn't like secret meetings or cleaning up after parties he had not attended. He didn't want to quit, so he just went inactive.

He had made close friends in ATO and rented an apartment with another ATO computer engineering student named Vince. They shopped for food at Wegmans, where Vince's younger brother worked. Chris met a high school girl named Michelle, who worked in the bulk food department, and he asked her out. She told him she was sorry, but she already had a boyfriend and gave him some broken cookies. He would stop there once a week, and finally, one day, Michelle said, "I broke up with my boyfriend." The rest is history.

Four years later, we attended the Baccalaureate program at Syracuse, sitting in the balcony with Michelle and her parents; Chris was with us. A young man approached us and said, "Chris, you are supposed to be on the stage. You are receiving some awards." Sheepishly, he made his way to the stage.

Since he was a graduate student, he did not want to attend graduation with the undergraduates. Later, he discovered that he was supposed to be a part of the group leading the students into the arena. Chris was named a Syracuse Scholar!

Michelle was headed off to Oswego for college, having graduated as valedictorian of her high school class. We all loved her from day one, and five years later, they married.

They have three daughters fluent in French, Spanish, and English. They speak only French with Chris, Spanish with their nanny, and English with their mom, who also jumps in on the French.

I started them all with riding lessons. The circle continues.

CHAPTER 42

1988 · Whirling TV & Calculating Cookies

Experimenting was a favorite pastime of our son, Chris. When he was two, he created his first test study using a pacemaker magnet my husband had brought home from the hospital. These gigantic magnets are used to insert or restart a pacemaker at the hospital, and then they are discarded. The magnet has a hole in the center about three inches in diameter, primarily blue, like a donut. Chris had used it to pick up everything metal he could, including some smaller trucks. He tried the larger vehicles, realized they would not hold, tried the medium-sized, and was satisfied with them as a toy.

We had just moved to a new home after two years in the Army and furnished our house. We purchased a 24-inch color television in a walnut cabinet, probably about $300, in 1971.

Chris was playing quietly, not unusual for him. His sister, Kim, was in school, and he was used to being alone with me. My husband came home for lunch, a perk of living in a small town, and Chris was very excited to show him what he had learned. He took him by the hand and said, "Daddy, come!" he led him to the TV. Though the child wanted to watch something, Daddy turned it on. "Daddy, look," Chris said as he swirled the pacemaker magnet around the screen in a large circle. The pixels were attracted to the lure creating a swirl of color. The sound was still on, but the picture was gone. Chris was delighted with his discovery.

 I called the store where we had bought the TV, and the salesperson said, "I never heard of anything like this. I will call Motorola and get back to you." The solution came back within the hour. "Turn the TV off, and the pixels will re-align. You have a budding scientist on your hands."

MY DADDY DID IT

When Chris was younger, a babysitter called my husband at the hospital and asked him to come right home. Chris had fallen and hit his head in a corner, bleeding. Eddie ran home, let the sitter go, and took Chris back to the hospital with him, where he worked as a general surgeon. Expertly he sewed up the cut on Christopher's head and put a bandage over it. Chris had a teddy bear with him, and the nurse asked if Chris would like Teddy to have a band-aid. He was delighted that he and Teddy would match.

On the way home, they stopped at the grocery store. A woman smiled at Chris, who was in the cart's seat, and said, "Oh my, what happened to your forehead?" Chris looked like a Botticelli angel with the sweetest smile and a head full of blond curls. He looked at her and proudly announced, "My daddy did it!"

HIS COLLECTION

At about age four, Chris began dismantling discarded electronic devices and keeping some parts. His bed had two huge drawers underneath, and he filled them with a tangle of wires. He would go through his collection when he needed parts for a new project.

A SHINY CIRCLE

My husband is an avid hunter. He likes guns and has instructional books all about gun safety. He reloads his shells and has a complete lab for doing so. Chris, age seven, was in the basement with him. He asked for some shots to look at before and after the reloading. He quietly sifted the gunpowder from several shells and created a pattern on the cellar floor and his design was circular with a tail at the bottom. He was thrilled that the fire followed the pattern. "Daddy, come and look at this." He lit the bottom with a match and cried, "I discovered it!"

Chris is 50 now, and the design is still visible, burned into the cellar floor.

AN INTERESTING GAME

Some friends from the medical school years invited us for a birthday dinner. Their son, Greg, who was five years older than Chris, had an electronic game, and he generously let Chris play with it. We had to tear him away to get him to go home, long past his bedtime. Within two days, we had located 101 Things You Can Do With Electricity and bought it.

HOW TO GET AN EMAIL ADDRESS

As he became more interested in science, we enrolled him in summer programs at Union College in Schenectady, New York. The first was rocketry, and they used computers to make their plans. Chris wanted to continue working on this at home, so he stood behind the office secretary and watched her put in her password. He used it in the evening to continue his rocket planning. He was called into the office and asked how he had entered the school's computer the night before. When he told them how much he wanted to work on his rocket at home, they let him off with a scolding. The secretary changed her password.

JUST DO ME A FAVOR

We attended a demonstration at Apple Computers. Joe Fischetti described VisiCalc as a forerunner of Microsoft Works, Quicken, Lotus, and Excel. He was an engineer in the large appliances division at General Electric and the father of two. This speaker was so clear that I, who do not have a mathematical mind, understood him. I spoke to him after the lecture and asked him to take Chris as a student. He declined, saying that he did not want to take more students. He had just finished with a young man leaving for college and enjoyed more time for himself.

I continued to call him intermittently for a year. Finally, I said, "Please, try him for one hour. I will stop calling you if you don't want to teach him."

We took Chris to Joe's house, and they went downstairs. What seemed like hours later, they came back up and Joe, the teacher, said, "Well, you were right; I want him as a student."

Thus began a friendship between student and teacher that would last a lifetime. We dropped Chris at Joe's house every Friday night for the next seven years. He learned to program and repair his equipment.

MAKING HIS OWN GAME

Chris had the first portable computer made by a company called Compaq. It was about ten inches thick and two feet by three feet with a handle, which was the only thing that made it portable. Chris would make it talk, and the computer would often call his sister. "Kim, Kim, Kim, come in here right now." It had a noisy dot matrix printer, and he spent most of his time in his room working on it.

By this time, Kim was a freshman in college, and Chris was in eighth grade. She had to do a research study on the permutation of

Latin Squares for statistics class. Chris set his computer to run the analyses, which ran continuously for the entire Christmas break. I can't remember the results, but I certainly remember the noise.

HORSES

I taught riding, and at the end of each summer, I took the students on a trail ride one day and another to a horse show. Chris came along as a groom, and he enjoyed the girls' company. Shelley, one student, was older than Chris but very petite and pretty. The horse shows took place at the county fair. We put the horses in the trailer with water and hay when the competition was over and went to the midway. Chris and Shelley climbed into a car on the whirl-a-gig ride. Shelley looked and said, "And don't think you are going to slide up against me on this ride." Chris laughed and said, "Shelley, centrifugal force will throw me to the outside, not up against you."

Chris did not lose his love of computers and science and continues to work as a computer engineer at Facebook.

During his college years, Chris spent a great deal of time with his Michelle, his girlfriend, who was beautiful. They are married now, and many years ago, they were flying to Michigan for his grandmother's 90th birthday. At the airport, they bought cookies.

Chris and Michelle were having a scientific conversation about the cookies they had bought at the airport. Chris had one giant cookie, and Michelle had one slightly smaller. Once they were on the plane, Chris said more fat was in her smaller cookie than in his large one. They had eaten the cookies, but they still had the wrappers. They took out the papers and measured the grease spots. Michelle pointed out that Chris's cookie had been much thicker than hers; his was four inches across while hers was only three-and-a-half. He took a pencil and wrote that the area of a circle is pi*r^2. Michelle took

Chris's pencil and pointed out that radius (r) is only half the width, so the difference wasn't that big. She went on to say that pi didn't matter; since Chris's cookie was twice as thick, Michelle's cookie would have had to be wider by a factor $\sqrt{}$ (radical two). She wasn't finished. Next, Michelle pointed out that using $\sqrt{}$ (radical two), her cookie would have needed to be almost five-and-a-half inches across to have compensated for the difference. Chris conceded defeat, but not without a bit of a thrill at the fact that his girlfriend knew the value of $\sqrt{}$ (radical).

FRANCE

A few years later, they moved to France for a year. Chris convinced Michelle to pack everything in cube-shaped cardboard boxes he had purchased at Staples. He believed this would provide the most volume for packing while staying within the airline's rules that a suitcase had to be <160 inches. He calculated that squares would give them the maximum space, and they bought cardboard boxes. He was delighted with this plan.

During their three-hour layover on the flight to Paris, the boxes were rain-soaked, and the plan had not included rain in London.

SABRINA AT FIVE

Chris and Michelle regularly estimate the volume of cookies to calculate how much insulin they will need to give their second daughter, Sabrina, who has juvenile diabetes. Michelle serves Sabrina and her two sisters the exact, measured, calculated dinners. The doctors and nurses who worked with Chris and Michelle were amazed and impressed at how they garnered any information they could find about Sabrina's care. No one was hungry, and no one felt that she was different.

CHAPTER 43

1990 · Our Names Are Mud

WE CAN NEVER GO HOME

I had an exercise routine, walking three days a week with my friend Diane until the year that she went back to work. I returned to the gym, and Diane and I squeezed in a workout weekly. Diane said on one of these workouts, "I have a week off and no place to go, but I wasn't planning on spending a lot of money" A light bulb went on in my brain.

"I have always wanted to organize a trip. Teachers lead student trips every summer. You and I could plan an adult trip while I am president of the Friends of the Library. We can earn one trip paid in full for every six attendees. I am sure we can interest 12 library members to join us."

Diane's answer: "Let's go to London! We speak the language!"

I cleared it through the Library Director and the board of the Friends. We chose a group named EF tours, which advertised adult groups. Their literature looked good, and the price was undoubtedly within our budget. We added $100 per person for the library.

Amsterdam is a small town, and the world travels fast. We set a date inviting anyone interested to meet at the library and went to work, choosing a week at the beginning of October and writing our advertising. Twenty-six people showed up. We were *delighted*.

Everyone signed up! My friend, Katie, decided to send her mother, and my sister, Janet, called to say she would come. The average age was 65. We were younger and could easily match the energy of people that age. We hired Brown's Bus, a local company, to transport us to JFK. They picked us up right on time at the Amsterdam Free Library. Everyone was excited, and we were impressed to see how very well-dressed they were. We served wine and cheese, small desserts, and a gift of a tiny journal for the trip. Diane, Janet, and I never slept on the flight. We had drinks and talked and laughed. Diane is an only child and never knew how much fun it was to have sisters.

BARRY, THE GAY GRUMPY GUIDE

Our tour guide, Barry, met us at the airport, and it was early morning. It was too early to go to our hotel, and the bus would keep our luggage. Our first stop was Trafalgar Square, and after a walk around the outside, posing for photos of Nelson's Column and the National Gallery, it was lunchtime in the US, and people were hungry. Barry suggested we go to the Crypt of St. Martin in the fields. It was perfect. The crypt has beautiful vaulted ceilings and historic tombstones. It was inexpensive, and the food was excellent.

During lunch, Barry confided in several women that he was gay and would like to show us where he lived in SoHo. He said there were many stores there for them to shop. These ladies did not realize that they might be shopping for whips and chains, so we had to rein Barry in, and he didn't like it, nor did he like me. Uh-Oh, that was just the beginning. We wandered for a few hours and took photos with the flower sellers, reminiscent of *My Fair Lady*.

Wembley is a lovely town, safe as anywhere can be. The central station in Wembley affords travel anywhere in London. Our hotel staff was amicable and very young and caused us one error. Our rooms were not ready, and we were not surprised. Six of us wanted to return to London for dinner. Everyone else decided to stay in Wembley, and they enjoyed a typical English dinner and tour of the little town. They loved their British restaurant and enjoyed unpacking leisurely. Dinner was included in our package, and we had rail passes. It was beginning to get dark as we approached London. The escalator seemed interminable, as the trains are very deep. We were welcomed to London by a maze of lights, taxis, and noise. Piccadilly Circus is well named and a fantastic place to begin our trip.

Dinner took place in Pizza Land. We had vouchers for 21 and were only seven. We asked for an upgrade, and they said we could eat all we wanted. We had extra vouchers a few times and wondered if Barry was getting a kickback. What happened to the additional coupons? The pizza was terrific, and the place underground would have been good for teenagers. We found a bus home instead of the subway, and it was heaven. By now, we were exhausted and wanted a shower and a bed. Janet had a single room, and Diane and I shared. We are clothes horses; we unpacked and put our outfits together. We had packed well, and our photos prove it. We were impressed with our group and how they looked.

On our first morning, we found a small cardboard box outside our room with a tea bag, sugar, a muffin, and a kit to make coffee for a small breakfast.

The coach picked us up for a London tour and a Windsor trip. The weather was perfect for October. We sat on the hill by Windsor

Castle and enjoyed the spectacular changing of the guard. The uniforms were stunning.

THE GYPSIES & MARY ANN

Windsor is a lively little town with restaurants and shops galore. Lunch was on our own, and we found a lovely pub, and most of the group chose it. We sat down for lunch, and Sylvia, who had lived in London, suggested we try a shandy. It combines beer and lemon/lime soda and is refreshing.

Three young people entered the restaurant and brought attention to themselves when one of them hit his head on the ceiling.

 A sign below said MIND YOUR HEAD, and they were laughing about it. They were beautiful young people with pale faces and dark black hair. We were all admiring them. The young man dropped his raincoat on the floor as we all looked on. He retrieved it, and they left. We finished a lovely lunch and were anxious to shop for gifts when Mary Ann shrieked, "My purse is gone!" We immediately realized that the gorgeous young man had picked it up when he dropped his coat. I asked Diane and Janet to run outside and look at the trash barrels' tops. They began looking for her purse and then; looked at each other and asked, "Why did we do as she said?" Not only did Mary Ann have her passport and ticket in her purse but she also had the photocopies.

WOE IS ME

Two days later, Mary Ann and Barry spent a morning at the American Embassy.

We visited St. George's Chapel in Windsor, where our guide, Godfrey, told the story of the Church of St. James in Windsor and spoke of the history of each section. At the last spot, Godfrey invited us to sit near the crypt, and he told us the story of Elizabeth Woodville.

As Americans, the word "woes" means something troublesome. Godfrey told us that this was his favorite spot. He said, "Elizabeth was married to Edward York, whose family crest was the White Woes. She was referred to as The White Queen."

We were all looking at each other in confusion when he showed us a burial coffin of a queen who was called the White Rose. When we reached the crypt, and it was marked with a white rose, understanding dawned. Janet broke up, leaned over to me, and said, "I wove you."

Our bus tour ended at an outdoor market, where we made a quick run-through for souvenirs. Who could resist the department store Fortnum & Mason? Diane bought a fantastic hat she would wear to tea at the Dorchester. We chose food-type gifts to bring home and hated to leave. But it was getting late, so we opted for dinner at a small pub around the corner.

BEGGING & BARGAINING WITH A LONDON TAXI DRIVER

A few women wanted to return to the hotel and did not want to brave the subway. Being a New Yorker, I stepped outside and hailed a cab. The driver did not want to go to Wembley, nor did the next cabbie. We hailed a third beautiful London taxi, long and sleek, with two jump seats inside. Unlike the New York city drivers, the London drivers are gentlemen.

This time I said, "Hi, I would like to ask you a question, Sir. What would make you happy enough to drive these tired American ladies to Wembley?" We agreed on £25, about $5 each, and the women were climbing in. London taxis are lovely. We had four squeezed in the seat, and two jump seats were in front of that. I pressed the last woman, pushing her up the high step by her substantial bum, when the driver said quietly to me, "Don't you have anyone smaller?"

THE RADIATOR CAP HAS GONE MISSING

We had a free day and chose to travel to Bath. When I called the hotel from the US weeks ago, I asked for the concierge, who told me he could arrange travel for us, a round trip to Bath. The price was right per person. Grace and her husband had owned their own large bus company for years, so she was the first person to raise her eyebrows when two vans with 13 seats each were waiting for us. These were used for school trips, and the windows were low for the children. Everyone was game to go. Even though we had not expected this form of transportation, 15 miles into the trip, our "buses" piled into a large, modern gas plaza. We told everyone to take a quick break. As they left, the driver said to me that there was a problem with the larger van. "The radiator cap has gone missing," our driver explained. "We can make it to Bath and have it fixed there. Every 15 miles, we had to pull over to the side of the road. One woman, Antonella, was seated over the engine. She had to leave her seat, each time, and wait outside while they filled the radiator with water. In this way, we limped into Bath, which did not disappoint.

Everyone was on their own, and most chose a lovely tour of the Roman Baths. We ate what they called a Ploughmans lunch at a pub and climbed the hill to see some posh apartments called The Circus, built in a crescent shape. The view was spectacular. We found a costume museum nearby. I bought a set of English bone china for my dollhouse. We were all dressed in layers and topped with raincoats, so we were warm enough in the fall weather. It only rained once on the trip, somewhat of a miracle in England.

Meanwhile, a magnificent sight was on the bus's left, so we called everyone's attention to the beautiful lush green pasture with about 100 sheep. By that time, we had reached the top of the hill, and the bus went on to Stonehenge, where the history was chilling. Our next stop was to be Salisbury cathedral, and we had two staunch

Episcopalians on our trip who were planning this as the highlight. When we returned to the car, our drivers had bad news for us. They thought it was very late to include Salisbury cathedral. "We can't let one group go there, and the other goes back. We must keep the cars together if one breaks down," we were told. Our dinner was planned at a restaurant on the Thames, and it was already 6:00 p.m. I gathered our group in the parking lot and explained the situation. I asked them to vote. The vote was to return to London and the reservation for dinner on the Thames at 7:00 p.m. I telephoned Barry using the driver's phone and said we would be late, arriving at about 8:00 p.m. He threw one of his tantrums and claimed that the restaurant would not accommodate us. Diane had been listening and grabbed the phone from me, and in powerful language, she told Barry to get food and drink for 26 people and bring it to the hotel by 8:30 p.m. "We will meet you at the hotel, and you had better have dinner for us," she added. That night Margot, one of the Episcopalians, bought me a drink and let me off the hook.

PIMENTO & PIES

We were happy to be back and had enjoyed the day despite the vans. Diane was in charge of the money, and she paid the drivers, telling them she did not feel that they lived up to their contract and they had caused us to miss Salisbury and our dinner. She informed them that we would pay half the agreed amount, and they graciously accepted it. The hotel gave us a room, and Barry arrived, bringing Pimento cheese sandwiches and five frozen lemon meringue pies. Mae Rira, our southern belle, put the fork into her pie, and lemon meringue squirted out and landed on Dolores, who dropped her drink on herself, and she began to laugh as did everyone else, but it was more like hysteria. When Diane and I returned to our room, I closed the door and leaned against it, blurting out, "Our names are mud, and we can never go home. You will go to work, and I will have to face the town alone."

THE RAVENS & THE WHEELCHAIR

The Tower of London! What a fantastic place. The line was around the corner when we arrived, and we gasped. I saw a sign for groups to enter and ran to the window and bought 26 tickets with my credit card. There was no line for groups, and he had plenty of time. We borrowed a wheelchair for an older member of our group named Jean. I pushed her over the cobblestones with the sun shining on the ravens living by the tower.

I HATE AND FEAR BIRDS, and I had read many novels of England describing how the ravens dug out people's eyes. The crown jewels were on the second floor. Diane took over pushing Jean. She went through and left Jean to shop. A long line had formed to see the jewels. The guard realized that Diane was responsible for Jean in the chair. He put his arm across the crowd and waved her in. There is kindness when you least expect it.

The Tower is indescribable, and one must see it all to appreciate living there. It reminds me of the history that had taken place there. The guards were wonderfully gracious. I skipped the torture chambers because I couldn't get the wheelchair down the steps.

London Bridge is down the hill from the Tower, and we took a trip on the Thames to the Embark and the British Museum. The Rosetta Stone was in the lobby. You could pose by it, photograph your group, and touch it. This is not so today.

GREEN DINNER & HUMBLE PIE

As usual, our dinner was inedible, but this time, I let the owner have it. They served us green food. It was a pub, so many of our group bought a different dinner. Our bus for the theater arrived, and we spent a long while waiting for two women, Mae Rita and Kay. I asked Barry if he knew anything, and he said they had gone to meet Kay's son for the evening. I gave him some snotty answer, and he went off on me and got in the bus. He took the mike as we drove to the theater. "Robin thinks she is a tour guide, and she is NOT. There has been no communication with your group. I am leaving you, and she can take over." Barry had all our tickets and vouchers, so I walked up and sat next to him and placated him until he agreed to stay. As I returned to my seat, Sylvia leaned over and whispered, "You have had steak and kidney pie and shepherd's pie, and now you have eaten humble pie."

The bus dropped us at the theater. The play was terrific, so scary that when Janet let out a blood-curdling scream, our youngest traveler, Trish, who was sitting in front of us, jumped over the seat and landed on the floor.

Our driver returned. Barry had left us for the night, and the driver brought us back to the pub where he picked us up. We talked quietly to him. He did not know how to get to Wembley, but Sylvia did. She sat next to him, and together, they got us there. Barry had never told him we were to go back to Wembley.

The following day, rested and fed, we took cabs to Harrods because it was raining, and we all planned to meet at 4:00 p.m. at the Dorchester hotel, where I had made arrangements for tea. It was beautiful and scrumptious.

After devouring our cardboard box breakfast one morning, we set off to the Victoria and Albert Museum. Diane took the group, and I ordered a cab and took Barry and Mary Ann to the American Embassy to get her new passport. The group went to Parliament and Big Ben, then jumped on the Tube to Westminster and High

Halloran to a pancake restaurant where everyone enjoyed all types of filling for the crepes.

FIRE IN THE MORNING

In the morning, as we dressed, a fire alarm went off, and we were herded to the parking lot. I sat on a curb and finished pulling my tights on. Antonella said, "I bet you didn't know this was so much work."

Barry could have made it easier. We finally heard that he was fighting with his partner.

When we went to the airport on our last day, we would part from Barry.

We had agreed the day before that we would cut Barry's tip, which was generous, and use the difference for the Tower of London.

I asked the group, "Does everyone agree that we should do this?"

One of the few men on the trip, Don Fabozzi, said, "I have a tip for him. Tell him to get out of the business."

We got everyone through customs, separated ourselves from our luggage, and went to our gate. We had one hour to relax.

ANNOUNCEMENT

"Will Jean Sutch please return to the desk." I got up and said, "I will go."

After I was gone, someone said, "Oh no, what if she runs into Barry?"

I didn't, and when I got to the desk, the agent said she could not give me Jean's purse holding her passport. I leaned over the desk and said to her, "I have taken 26 senior citizens on a week's tour of London. Everything that could go wrong did go wrong. Jean Sutch is in a wheelchair. Please, please give me her things. And she did!"

A week or so later, I received a scathing letter from Barry. This time he was not getting away with it. I called EF, gave them a run-down of how he had let us down, and read them the letter. They assured me that his job as a guide was over.

I had a party to exchange photos, and everyone came.

CHAPTER 44

1997 · Declan Had a Daddy Named Joe

Kim and Joe lived in an apartment house on the west side in New York City. They designed a room for the baby, and they began to think about the boy's names. Every day, Joe would try a different name. Kim said, "Go into the baby's room and talk to a make-believe baby and try out a different name each time." Joe would go into the nursery, the new room for the baby. "Hi, Sean."

On September 27, Declan was born. Joe took Kim to Lenox Hill Hospital. Everyone was very excited. Joe helped Kim breathe deeply, and the doctor and nurses were all there to help. Pretty soon, Joe and Kim had new names. They were *Mommy* and *Daddy*. They took Declan home to their apartment and put him into his new crib.

Daddy drove Declan and *Mommy* to *the faraway house* two weeks later, and Declan was christened in Saint Mary's Church. *Daddy* held him during the christening while Father Gulley, *Mommy's* special friend, said the prayers.

After a party at the Union Hall Inn, *Daddy* stayed next to Declan's bassinette because he did not want people to take Declan out and carry him around. He put his little arms over his head and looked like an actor baby in the movies.

Declan grew and grew. He had a small football, and *Daddy* would put it under Declan's arm and run with him. Declan would laugh, and when they were finished, they took a nap in *Daddy's* big brown chair.

When it was Declan's first birthday, *Daddy* and *Mommy* stayed home from work and took Declan to the park and played all day. They went home and ate some cake and Declan liked it very much. *Daddy* loved the cake, and he ate three pieces.

Daddy and *Mommy* took Declan on trips to the faraway house or to visit Nana Pat at her house. Sometimes, Grammy would ask *Mommy*, "Where is Joe?" *Mommy* would say, "He is with Declan inside." Daddy liked to spend time alone, just whispering to his little son.

Soon the new house was ready, and a big moving truck came and took everything to the new house. It was a big house with a large backyard. *Mommy* and *Daddy* had many plans for swing sets and sandboxes in that yard for Declan.

Declan and *Daddy* liked to mop the floors in the new house together. *Mommy* and Declan wanted to play walk the doggie. *Mommy* would lay down on the floor, and Declan would pull *Mommy* by her hair and slide her along the shiny wood. There was no furniture in the living room and dining room yet.

When *Daddy* went to work, Declan would wave bye-bye to him from the family room window, and when it got dark, he went to the same window to wait for *Daddy* to come home. After dinner at night and after his bath, Declan and *Mommy* would read a story. Then *Daddy* came to the gate and said, "The prince of darkness is here." He would take Declan to his nursery and rock him while he drank his bottle and fell asleep.

On a sorrowful day in January, Declan was waiting by the window. *Mommy* came and took his hand and said, "I will put you to bed tonight because I have a new story to read to you."

After the story, Declan falls asleep in the Rocking Chair.

The doorbell rang, and it was the police telling *Mommy* the terrible news that Joe had died in an auto accident.

Everyone came to stay with Declan and *Mommy*. Declan was 16 months old. *Mommy* was 34.

CHAPTER 45

2000 · No Good Deed Goes Unpunished

"We have to get to the Hockney exhibit at the Met this week," I told my husband. "OK, say when?" was his response. "Tomorrow," I commanded.

"The exhibit was fantastic, colorful, and fun," I told my daughter on the phone. "We are on the train now and will be there in one hour for the game. See you then. I am on Dad's phone. I lost mine yesterday."

I gave the phone back to Eddie, "I think I left it at the Met yesterday when you were photographing the two women. They aren't open yet, but I will call from Kim's house."

When we arrived at Kim's, her first words were, "Your phone is at the Metropolitan. I tried to call you, and the woman answered and said you could pick it up at the office anytime. Why did you have your phone out in the museum?"

"I noticed something beautiful happening. A mother and daughter sat on the front bench, admiring a painting. The mother was in a wheelchair, and the daughter was leaning over her mom's shoulder to discuss the Hockney painting. They put their heads close together and whispered. I tapped Daddy on the shoulder and said, 'Isn't that a lovely scene?'"

"He walked over to them and asked if he could take their picture. That became an event. They wanted to pose in front of one painting and then the other. The mother said she was 93 and didn't usually agree to take her picture in her wheelchair. Dad and the women had such an interesting dynamic that I took my phone out to photograph the scene. I must have put it down on the bench. I became involved in the conversation. I didn't miss it until this morning, and we had to catch the train. I am glad to know that it is safe."

We attended our grandson's hockey game and returned home the next day. I immediately set out for the Metropolitan Museum to retrieve my phone. I always listen to a book on tape while running around the city. I was so involved in the story of Janet Auchincloss and her daughters, Jacqueline Kennedy and Lee Radziwill, that I did not see the uneven sidewalk ahead of me. I fell hard, landing on my face. I felt my nose give. Some lovely people stopped immediately to help me, but I knew better than to let them pull me up. I needed to assess the damage. They offered to get me a cab to go home, but

I was just a few blocks from the museum, and I wanted my phone. I decided I could do it and walked slowly and carefully in a daze to the museum, retrieved my phone, and meticulously descended those steps to a cab and home. I never saw myself in a mirror. The doorman asked if I was OK and then asked if my husband was home. I later found out that he had been an EMT. I got to the apartment and walked in, and burst into tears. "I fell," I said. Eddie immediately went to a medical professional character to assess the damage, give me some pills, and settle me on the couch. I slept soundly with ice on my face, and he woke me every two hours to ensure I was OK. I had no intention of going to the emergency room. Three days later, I attended my writing class by taking a cab there and back. Everyone was sympathetic.

I might have a broken wrist because it was excruciating. "You should go to the emergency room! The nurses will look at your bruised face, and you will go to the head of the line," said my class-mates. I left class at 1:20 p.m., took a cab to the Cornell-Weill emergency room, and asked them to X-ray my wrist. The ER doctor saw me immediately and sent me for X-rays and a CAT scan of my head.

In half an hour, they had me signed up for x-rays, and within 45 minutes, I was in the wheelchair and on my way to the x-ray department, where they were quick, thorough, and pleasant. Someone returned me to the emergency room to wait for the radiologist to discuss my x-rays with me.

I waited for half an hour and then asked if my x-rays had been read and was told that they were there and that the radiologist would be here soon. He was someone I had seen in the room the entire time. I was there, and he kept looking at me. He called me into a private room and said that some blood showed in the CAT scan of my brain and that they had to send me to the emergency room that handled more critical things. Since this scared me, I called my husband. It was 4:00 p.m., and he came to the hospital and met me in an emergency room where I was given a bed in a hallway filled with other patients. I sat in my jeans and sweatshirt, waiting to see a physician. I informed them that my husband was a retired general surgeon, and soon, a neurosurgeon showed up and told me that they should admit me for the night so they could watch me and wake me up every two hours. They were insistent and sent a general surgery resident to talk to me. He and my husband agreed that I did not need to be admitted since it was four days since the fall, and the bleeding was so minimal that it should be reabsorbed by the morning. My husband agreed to wake me every two hours and ensure I was alert.

RETURN OF THE NEUROSURGEON

It was now 5:30 p.m. I arrived at 2:00 p.m. The neurosurgeon insisted that I be admitted, so we agreed. Promising he would be back in a little while, he returned at 7:00 p.m. to tell me that they would send me to the trauma section and that now I was dismissed from neurosurgery. At 8:00 p.m., the surgeon from the trauma section, who had already agreed that I should go home, came to see me and said that the neurosurgeon insisted that I be admitted. He would talk to his chief and come back. In the meantime, I was not without entertainment because across the hall from me was a small room with an older woman in the bed wearing a hospital gown and nothing else.

She was hard of hearing, so I was privy to everything the doctor said across the hall. They first told her that she had pneumonia and would have to be admitted. They later told her there was a problem with her heart rate, and she would have to be admitted. They did a complete verbal admission questionnaire, which included everything from how often she walked in a day to how often she had a bowel movement and whether they were well-formed.

In the meantime, her two daughters and granddaughter arrived. They had gone to the cafeteria and returned with soup. I was starving, and I could smell their soup. It smelled delicious until the old woman said, "Oh, I'm going to have diarrhea."

She did!

I could not only see it but also hear and smell it. While the nurses were cleaning up the patient, the African American man in the next bed to me was being questioned by another physician and asked the same questions. Now I know everything I need to know about his bowel movements, how they were formed, and what was causing his pain. He then got on his iPhone and began conversing with everyone in his family. At first, he was relatively quiet, but soon he began to speak more loudly. We guessed he was possibly a preacher because he was quoting the Bible and excerpts of a sermon about being delivered. I had one heck of a headache, and I went to the desk and asked what the plan was for where they were putting me. At 9:00 p.m., the surgeon came back with the head of the department and agreed that I could go home and not be admitted to the trauma department. The female physician said, "I have two things I need to do before I can discharge you."

In about an hour, I saw the general surgery resident at the end of the hall and hoped that he was now coming to give me some discharge papers; however, he went in and out of two rooms and left the floor. I went back to the desk and asked the nurse what was going on, and she said she would page my doctor. Again, I returned to the counter, and she said he was not answering. At 10:30 p.m., I returned to the front desk and said, "I am going home."

"You cannot go; you still have an IV set up in your arm."

"My husband is a physician. He will remove the IV for me when we get home."

"I'm sorry you had to wait so long, and I'll be happy to remove the IV for you since I know it is uncomfortable."

She did, and we walked home, arriving at 11:00 p.m. The British have a particular word for this: Gobsmacked.

I should not finish this story without explaining that I live in a small town in upstate New York, where my husband practiced surgery for 30 years. If I walked into the emergency room there, I would be given the royal treatment, taken immediately, and if the doctor said he was coming back, he would come back. I had heard emergency room stories before and never really believed them, but I will never again go to the emergency room. If I can't see a personal physician, I will go to a walk-in clinic on Third Avenue, where I can watch everyone in the one space, and they can't disappear the way the other doctors were doing.

CHAPTER 46

2001 · Beating Cancer

I was relieved to return to my own home with my children, my special daughter-in-law, and my beloved two-year-old grandson, who seemed to know something was wrong. As soon as I sat down, he approached me cautiously, walking the length of the couch, putting his arms around my neck, and he kissed me, the best medicine.

Francine, a dear friend, is a healer, and she taught me how to meditate and reach my spirit guides. I arranged a circle of spirit guides all in heaven now. I included my mother and father, Joe Fine, my son-in-law who had just recently died and whom I loved dearly, my friend Carol from high school, my uncle Joe, the patriarch of our family, Aunt Helen, Aunt Gertrude, and my Aunt Anita. I imagined them in heaven in a circle. I'm not sure this is what Francine meant by spirit guides, but I decided they would be mine. When I went to bed at night, I would call them up. I saw them as miniatures and would talk to them, tell them what I was worried about, and then listen for their answers. It was my meditation and highly therapeutic.

A lovely young nurse did my take-in admission forms. When she was finished, she told me that her mother and sister had breast cancer; she had bilateral mastectomies to avoid what they had gone through. "I will be happy to show you what you're going to look like." She did, and I was pleased with the look.

It is much easier to be the patient than it is to be the loved one standing by. Pretty soon, a nurse took me to a room gave me a gown and some meds to make me sleepy. The new thinking was that walking to the operating room made the patient feel in control. I had walked to the OR and climbed up onto the table for my biopsy, and I knew I was NOT in control, so I said, "I do not like this new idea of walking to the operating room, so please knock me out and take me there." I remember being in the waiting room outside the OR, and I decided that the best way to keep myself together was to follow my friend Katie's advice to repeat the Hail Mary over and over.

The next thing I knew, it was the middle of the night, and I woke up without too much pain. A woman in the next bed heard me moving, and she said, "I am here next to you. I had breast cancer surgery eight years ago, and the only reason I'm in the hospital now is that I have lymphedema, and I am here to treat that. Please feel free to talk if you want to. I am going to call the nurse to tell her that you are awake." The nurse came and knocked me out until the morning.

I looked around and realized that I was in a large room similar to a guest room in a country house. The furnishings and drapes were beautiful, newly decorated by Estee Lauder as a gift to the Memorial Sloan Kettering Cancer unit.

My mouth hurt. My doctor soon came to see me. She was almost at the end of her pregnancy, and she eased down into the comfortable chair. "You look pretty good for having had surgery yesterday, and if you were wondering about your mouth, it hurts because you went into respiratory arrest and the nurse had to intubate you immediately, giving you a fat lip."

"Thank God for that nurse," I thought.

Doctor Montgomery continued, "You had four positive nodes, which means that you will have the most potent chemotherapy, and you will lose your hair."

"My hair is the least of my worries." I replied.

Our son, Chris, came on the second day with his lovely wife, and they picked me up in their car at the front door of Sloan Kettering Memorial Hospital. I had lived in the same neighborhood at the age of 23, and when I had to be on York Avenue, I walked on the other side of the street from Sloan Kettering. I never wanted to be a patient there, but I was grateful for their work when I needed them, and I knew that I would have the best treatment possible. Somehow, they got me to the sidewalk and into the front seat of Christopher's car, and we drove the three blocks to our apartment house. Soon, I was upstairs in our sizeable pink chair. I did not want to be in bed.

The only discomfort was two necessary drains which would have to be pumped to remove excess fluid from the surgical sites. Fortunately, my physician husband was able to handle the drains. I could get dressed in loose shirts that were buttoned. I could not put anything over my head, but about day six, I began to put on makeup—always a good sign.

We walked to the plastic surgeon's office for my first fill. After the mastectomies, a plastic surgeon puts in a saline expander. Dr. Cordeiro had completed this part, and the expanders would be filled once a week using a needle. There was a slight pain at once, and muscle pain later as the expanders did their job stretching the muscles under which implants would be placed. They had no shape and would be removed later in an implant exchange, a quickie surgery.

Emille, my college roommate, came to New York from Puerto Rico when I had my third fill. I put on a suit with a very short skirt and a Gucci scarf, and we went to lunch. She is always so cheerful and has improved my perspective.

The new implants were a very nice shape and size with no metal circle. I wanted to be smaller, and I was. When my sister, Janet, had the same drain a few years later, she called them her Judith Lieber bags, threw them over her shoulders, covered them with a scarf, and went to a wine tasting…how brave!

Follow-up mental therapy was with a beautiful group of women who had recently undergone the same surgery. The meetings were led by a social a social worker named Roz, who allowed no whining. We shared our problems and our fears. I went every three weeks when we traveled from Amsterdam to Manhattan for chemotherapy. We listened to *Harry Potter* tapes on those trips, and the author is a genius.

Eventually, the fear subsides. It has been 20 years! Thank you, God.

CHAPTER 47

2001 · The Hair on The Chair

The oncologist told me my hair would fall out three weeks after my first treatment. I began chemotherapy in June, and my hair began to fall out the week before the Fourth of July. My friend Debbie had told me to cut it when it started to fall out because she said hers came out in the shower and stuck all over her like snakes, and she began to scream.

Both children were home for the Fourth of July weekend; we celebrated at a friend's house. I felt a little nauseous, but nothing severe. I was enjoying myself out in the sunshine at the Wilsons' pool. Our children had grown up together and were delighted to see each other. I was sitting on a lawn chair that had a headrest. It was made of that plastic webbing, and at one point, I got up to get another soda. Chemotherapy is a powerful medication. NO ALCOHOL! My doctor was very strict about this and warned me. I followed all the rules as I had my whole life. Returning to my chair, I saw a large section of hair hanging from the webbing. It was so pretty, and the curls were still in it that I thought I could pin it back on for a minute. I realized I had to go home without making a fuss. No one had seen it. I managed to get the hair and put it into my pocket. The party was just about over anyway, and when we got back to our house, I took the hair out of my pocket and showed it to them. "Oh, mom, I am so sorry," said my daughter.

 I had no intention of being a whiny patient, so I said, "OK, today is the day it has to come off. Who wants to cut it?" We are a family that likes to do everything together, so they got a chair. Eddie stood behind me with Kim on one side, and my son, Chris, on the other. Armed with three pairs of scissors, they cut all my hair off, leaving me with a crewcut and the garbage can full of pretty, curly hair.

I am always prepared for makeup and hair, and I thought it might be a good idea to have a fun wig. I had always had long, brown hair with red highlights, so I bought a strawberry blonde short wig. After showering and scrubbing my head, I put on my nightgown, bathrobe, and a new wig. It was charming, and I felt better. I also had a long, brown wig, a gift from Kim, my daughter. So, my pretty hair was what I lost. I would learn later that I was never going to get it back.

I made it through chemotherapy and didn't need to write a story about that. My hair came back in a very dark gray color, but it was sparse. I continued to wear my wigs for several months until I had what I might've called a short shag.

We would take our grandson and his best friend, Michael, to the circus in the morning, and I was ready to go out without a wig. I bought a reddish-brown hair color that I had used before and colored my hair the way I had always done it. I couldn't wait to see myself with my hair. It was short, and after I rubbed it dry with a towel, I looked in the mirror and screamed. My hair was bright orange! I was ready for tomorrow's circus.

CHAPTER 48

2013 · Pitfalls of Parenting Viewed by Grandparents

The perfect trip to visit our grandchildren began with a tiny rolling suitcase containing everything in one space. Usually, we each have a shoulder bag, a suitcase, a carry-on with a book or iPad, and a plastic bag with lunch for the train. When we visit our three granddaughters in Boston, we pack lightly and use their well-equipped laundry room. We enjoy train travel and when we travel, we like to allow plenty of extra time. If the train is at 3:00 p.m., we want to leave the Upper East Side at 2:00 p.m. Depending on the traffic, it can take 15 minutes or 45 minutes by cab. Arriving at Penn Station, we locate a redcap and ask to be put onto the train as soon as it is ready. For a $5 tip per person you have a choice of location. We like the quiet car and a window seat on the side that runs along the northeastern shore. Having secured a promise from the redcap, I will go off searching for a picnic lunch, while my husband stays with the bags.

This plan went awry on Friday. We arrived at 2:30 p.m., and at 3:00 p.m., I was at Zaro's buying lunch when they announced that the Acela was boarding on track 11. I hastened back to the waiting room, where Eddie was frantically trying to call me on my cell phone. We got to track 11, and the escalator was coming up instead of going down. A guard informed us that we wanted to go to track 11 east. Running now, we barely made it to the Acela and could not find two seats together. "I guess we can't sit together," I said disappointedly, "but we can sit across the aisle from each other." A gentleman offered to move across the aisle, and we thanked him profusely and dug into our suitcases for my iPad and his book. "I'm so sorry," I said. "I thought the train was 3:30 p.m., not 3:15."

The woman in the seat in front of us knelt up on her chair and rudely announced, "This is the quiet car. Can't you two obey the rules?" Lowering my voice to a whisper, I said, "Sorry." The train doors were closing, and my husband wouldn't let it go, telling her that we would be happy to comply but that she could at least have asked nicely. She said, "I did the first time I asked you." Now, I couldn't leave it alone, and I whispered to her, "We are both hard of hearing. We didn't hear the first time."

We settled in for a lovely trip, some quiet reading, a good lunch, and a nap. Our daughter-in-law, Michelle, picked us up and gave us a choice to go to the house or pick up Annika at her school and go to gymnastics, where the older girls had a class. Of course, we chose Annika.

Chris and Michelle have three girls: Katya, nine; Sabrina, six; and Annika, three. The nine-year-old looks like a Kappler with the most fabulous dark curly hair. The six-year-old is the image of her mom, who is beautiful, and Annika looks like they went to Sweden and stole a child. She is as fair as a person with light blonde hair and blue eyes can be.

Everyone in this home speaks three languages. Chris and Michelle studied French and went to live in Paris when they were first married. When Katya was born, they planned to teach her French immediately. Michelle would speak only English to the children, and Chris would speak only French. If Katya talked to him in English, he would not answer except to remind her to speak French. They hired a Spanish nanny. We were unsure if it would work, but as tricky as it must have been, they persevered, and we now have three trilingual grandchildren.

On Saturday morning, we rose early to hustle children into car seats for a riding lesson at a barn near their home. After 15 years of listening to professionals teach our children and five years of teaching riding myself, I recognize that this teacher is exceptional. The barn was beautifully refurbished. The stalls are polished cherry with brick trim and black wrought iron fittings. The grooming and bathing area is brick with a rubberized floor and a central drain. To wash a horse, you use buckets of water with horse shampoo and scrub the horse from head to tail and under the tail! You rinse them with a hose, which they love in warm weather, scraping the excess water off with a sweat scraper. I enjoyed holding a newly bathed horse by a lead rope while they grazed and dried in the sun before being put away. The stalls are immaculate with new wooden shavings. Since they are within the city limits, they must truck the manure out of town.

Jen, the instructor, had asked our son if the girls could participate in a beginner horse show in May. Since he agreed, we were excited to take them shopping for jodhpurs, hunt coats, and blouses. Looking in the mirror, Katya said, "I am very pleased with the look of myself." Sabrina, is a quiet child about whom one could say, "Still waters run deep." She was diagnosed with juvenile diabetes in 2010, and she bravely accepts whatever comes next. She smiles at her image in the mirror and on our camera but doesn't say anything.

The older girls have swimming lessons, so we nap with Annika. We need it more than she does. Our last stop, at 5:00 p.m., is a Chinese restaurant. On the way there, the baby said, "My stomach hurts." We thought she might be carsick, and we were almost there. We all chose to eat dinner from the extensive buffet, and Chris and Michelle agreed that they would give Sabrina the usual amount of insulin and deal with the blood count later in the evening. Chris is a PhD in computer engineering, and Michelle has a master's in information systems. When they figure out carbs and insulin, we are relieved that Sabrina is in such good hands.

We all piled our plates and sat down at a round table against the wall. As Chris put his plate down, three-year-old Annika stood up on her chair and vomited onto her seat and the floor in one stream. Chris washed her up with the help of a Chinese waiter who must have children of his own and changed her into another set of clothing that they keep in their car. I am impressed with young fathers now who share so much of the responsibility. We all continued with our dinner, and Sabrina had a wonderful time choosing food and desserts as if she had no insulin dependence. She has a pump that she wears on a belt around her waist, and it is programmed to inject insulin over some time.

Michelle's cell phone rings, and we hear her say, "Oh no, I am so sorry. Since you are pregnant, you have to use vinegar and olive oil. I will text you the directions." Their babysitter has just discovered lice in her hair, and she cannot use the Mange medicine that the girls had used three weeks before when head lice ran rampant through Lexington's elementary schools. We are all finishing, and the waiter offers everyone ice cream. Annika seems to be enjoying hers and then turns to Chris and says, "My tummy hurts." in French. Chris picks her up and takes her outside just in time.

He does not want to let her vomit at the restaurant entrance, so he turns her toward himself, telling us later that he formed a chum bucket with his sweater. "Chum buckets are used on fishing boats to hold the remnants of fish," Chris explains. Michelle has paid the bill, and we return home in a smelly car. Michelle takes Annika upstairs for a bath.

Sabrina asks me to shorten the sleeves on her new horse-show blouse. The girls start a game on my iPad, and Chris sets up a magnifying lamp, taking them one at a time to go through their hair to see if the lice have returned. Since the sitter has them, they could come back. He sleeps in Sabrina's room and tests her blood levels every three hours, adjusting her pump as needed.

At Sunday breakfast with the baby better and Sabrina under control, the light shines on Katya. She has just received her ERB scores at nine, something like the SATS for fourth graders. This trilingual, computer-savvy swimmer, rider, and A student is upset about her scores. In the national norm, she is in the 99th percentile, suburban public schools 88th, and in independent schools in the 86th. All she can see is the 86th. She doesn't want to be in 86th and is making faces.

At 3:00 p.m., 36 hours after we left Penn station, we seat ourselves in the quiet car of the Acela from Boston's South station to New York's Penn station and wonder how we ever raised only two children.

CHAPTER 49

2015 · My Flying Horse
Annie Buttons

"Grammy," said my thirteen-year-old granddaughter, Katya, "I love jumping during my riding lessons. You are cantering around a ring, and you feel like you are flying, and then you go over the jump, and you are flying."

I have often had a dream that I could fly, but not far or high. It takes place in the hallway of my first home, an apartment in Park Slope in Brooklyn. I start slowly, then I am up, flapping my arms for a few minutes, and then I come down slowly.

Of course, I could not fly outside this dream, but Katya had just given me a description of how I could fly, and it brought me great pleasure. The horses I owned and trusted were Annie Buttons and Diamond B. John.

Annie had a quiet, unflustered personality and was a fearless palomino with a flaxen mane and tail. Diamond was a lovely, shiny chestnut with four white socks. He could jump to the moon but was afraid of anything new. I knew Annie from horse shows. She was a family horse and was consistent with both young and older riders.

To my surprise and delight, I met her again. She had been bought by Susan, a young girl who rode at the barn where Marsha, an alternate on the U.S. Olympic team, taught.

Marsha had been injured and returned to live on her family's farm for a while. I immediately called, and her mom, who told me they could take Kim as a student if she would be happy with a semi-private, which was all she had open. "I know you will like Susan," she assured me.

We agreed on the following Tuesday. When Susan arrived, I was surprised and happy. She was riding Annie Buttons! I had several months to observe Annie, and I loved her.

Six months later, Susan asked me for a private moment. With tears in her eyes, she told me that her family was moving, and she could not take Annie. "Give me a price," I said, "and I will buy her!"

I brought her home, and we immediately clicked. I rode her in the mountains, across wooden bridges, through glistening streams, and in the ring, where we practiced for horse shows. I showed her and won. I put children on her for lessons, and she would obey me from the ground. I put my students on her for horse shows, and they brought me back ribbons!

I bathed her, and she stood still while I scrubbed her and rinsed her with the hose. I bleached her mane and tail, being careful not to touch her skin.

My son Christopher rode her until he was ten, and with his beautiful blonde hair, they made an adorable combination, winning many ribbons, including a short stirrups championship.

I miss the pleasure of galloping her up hills. She was afraid of nothing. Riding is a pleasure of the past, which I can enjoy in retrospect, and I am grateful to have lived it and been lucky enough to find a horse that was the perfect match for me.

CHAPTER 50

2014 · Somewhere Over Seventy

Travel is exciting when all goes well. My friend Emille believes every vacation has one day of disaster. On February 14, I left on a trip so well-organized months in advance that nothing should go wrong. My youngest sister, Muffin, was turning 70 on Valentine's Day. We had been planning this Caribbean cruise for a while—just three sisters, no husbands, children, or grandchildren. The birthday girl was already 70 by the time we went to bed on Valentine's evening. I was hoping that this was the end of my vacation disaster day!

My car arrived on time at 6:30 a.m. and dropped me at the Delta terminal at JFK at 7:15 a.m. I checked in at the curbside and went straight to the gate. I always ask to pre-board as I need ten minutes to wrap my arm, which will swell in altitude change. As a good citizen, I removed my iPhone, turned it off, fell asleep on takeoff, and slept so soundly that the landing awakened me. I gathered my belongings in a sleepy stupor and deplaned. I used the courtesy phone for the hotel van and hurried to the baggage area. I knew my two sisters were already at the hotel. I was waiting for my bag and had that sinking feeling when you can't find something. Cruising requires clothing for formal evenings and glamourous days, and I was prepared. When my bag did not appear. I was directed to the baggage office. A gentleman was ahead of me, so I investigated my purse for the phone, thinking I would call my sisters and say I would be a little late.

OMG, my phone was not there. The clerk brought the man's bag from the back room, so I assumed she would do the same for me. However, when I showed her my baggage claim, I asked, "Could you possibly help me with my phone first? I am sure it is still on the plane. Can you call the gate?" "Of course. What seat were you in?" I responded, "12D," and asked her to ring my phone so the cleaning crew could find it. She promptly called the gate and was told my phone was not there in less time than it would have taken them to look.

One down, I can handle this, I think, and ask about my suitcase. "Your suitcase was routed to Bermuda. You may buy anything you need for tonight and save the receipts. Delta will reimburse you," she said and handed me a card with a phone number to call in about four hours.

Taking out my iPad, I went directly to the app that said, "Find my phone!" I was inside the airport. My driver had arrived from the hotel, and I proceeded to tell him my problems and show him the iPad locating my phone. He offered to return my coat and a small bag to the hotel with a reassuring smile and suggested I get security to go with me to reclaim my phone. I emailed my sisters to let them know what was happening. An hour running around that airport convinced me that phone insurance is worth the money you pay for it. The phone moved on the iPad locator, and I was sent from place to place and brushed off with less dignity than an iPhone deserves. Security officers would look at the iPad map and send me to another agent, who might say, "I am in training. Try gate D26 security desk." I won't say anymore as I am sure this is not an unusual experience. When the tears behind my eyes started to force themselves down my face, I found the exit and called the hotel van to come back for me. While waiting for the truck, I met two pilots and showed them the map, and they decided it was on a plane on the runway. Later that evening, I rechecked it, and it was at JFK. After that, I erased and locked it.

My driver arrived, all sympathy, which made me want to cry again because everyone so far has been unkind and annoyed! We arrived at the hotel, and my sisters ran out to hug me. They never got my email but heard the driver tell the front desk that there was a woman whose luggage was lost, and they guessed it was me.

I had paid for the room with Marriott miles, and they would not register my sisters without my credit card. They offered their own, but no go. They had to wait in the lobby.

We were together on our birthday trip, that was the most important thing. We stayed two days at this beautiful hotel. My sisters got dressed for dinner. Unfortunately, we are so differently-sized that I could wear nothing they have brought; we had to go shopping for me. A hotel van will take us to a mall, pick us up again, and take us to Hollywood Beach to see the circus on the Boardwalk. He can do it for $100, I slap a bill on the counter, and we are off in rush-hour traffic.

By the time we got to Hollywood Beach, it was dark. The birthday dinner was in a pizza place. Joe had given Janet money for the treat and wine, and we drank the entire bottle.

While we were at dinner, our cabin steward brought down a third bed out of the ceiling. It had a ladder swinging from it three feet above the floor; laughing hysterically, we tried to explain that not even Tarzan, at 70, could climb a swinging ladder and get out of bed three times a night to pee. The cabin steward called a supervisor, and together, they took the mattress off that bed and put the frame back into the ceiling. The mattress is more significant than the couch, hanging over three inches, and Janet spent the night sliding out. Our steward showed us a tiny bed beneath the sofa with a one-inch mattress in a drawer. It was smaller than a cot, and my turn to sleep on it. It was like putting a baby in a dresser drawer.

I could not take a deep breath in the morning because my ribs hurt so much. Without any steward, we finally figured out that this smaller mattress on top of the couch made a comfortable bed. Problem solved.

The first full day was a day at sea. My sisters headed to the hot tub. I wanted to evaluate the bathing suit I had pulled off a rack in Macy's without trying it on. It appeared to be a ruffled top to the waist and a separate skirted bottom with a wraparound skirt. However, the panty is not a brief but a bikini. This orange ruffled costume might look good on a 17-year-old but not for a 75-year-old Chiquita Banana. I did not take the tickets off; this will go back to Macy's. Forgoing the hot tub and pool, I spent the day in my Kmart shorts and a Fort Lauderdale t-shirt, reading and investigating the ship.

Janet and Muffin love the hot tub, and I discover that the ship's spa has an acupuncturist. I have wanted to try acupuncture for an I.T. band problem related to my hip replacement. A Brazilian-trained therapist was handsome and knowledgeable. I reserved him for every day at sea, and I am sure he can't distinguish Kmart from Chanel.

I wore the Macy's dress on the first formal night, which was not too bad. I will never wear it again, but Delta has said to buy what I need. They will pay for it, or I will give it to Goodwill.

San Juan, our first port, is historic and sunny! My luggage will arrive at the end of the day. I want to throw the Kmart outfit overboard. My college roommate, Emille, has lived in San Juan her whole life, has often been listed as the top best-dressed woman, and has appeared in many magazines. Too bad she moved to Connecticut two weeks before we arrived. She would have loved my white cotton Kmart skirt and probably hidden me from her friends.

The second port was St. Kitts, where we wanted to go to the beach; it did not disappoint, and soon we were floating in the lovely, clear green water at a sandy beach. We rented beach chairs from a University of Virginia graduate whose husband grew up in St. Kitts. They were taking a year off before getting jobs in the States. The people were pleasant and fun-loving.

My sisters are in the sea up to their necks, and I am happy reading a book under the umbrella in my bathing suit modestly fitting me.

The joke was on us in St. Maarten, where we hired a driver to show us the French and Dutch sides, including lunch and a beach. He informed us that the French give free homes to women from anywhere if they, legally or illegally, find a man and make a child. The man leaves, and the woman and child receive a salary and a house with no responsibility to work.

The driver, Simon, was from the Dutch side and disliked the French. He ranted about the French injustices against the Dutch for more than an hour. We had a nice lunch and shopped for some souvenirs in the markets. Our driver has promised to take us to a beautiful beach. The beaches are public; you can swim anywhere. There were three changing rooms with showers and stalls without locks. I chose the farthest of the three. Janet took the first, and while she was naked and trying to pull on her suit, a parrot walked in under the door, calling out, "Hello, hello!" The parrot's owner walked right in, grabbed the parrot, and put it outside. "I am so sorry," he said to a half-naked Janet. Two minutes later, Muffin looked down to see the parrot. Using an in-charge voice, Janet ordered, "Someone call this parrot. My sister is dreadfully afraid of birds!" They captured him and put him on a wall surrounding the dressing rooms. We could see and hear him, but he stayed put!

After getting rid of the bird, my sisters were ready to go into the water. I love to look at the water, not go into it. I offered to stay with our worldly goods on the beach, so they headed for the water. Meanwhile, the parrot follows me, talking his fool head off.

The first wave was so strong that it knocked Muffin over, then I saw Janet fall. Muffin got up only to be thrown down by another wave and crawled to the edge as her bathing suit filled with sand. They were back instantly, wanting to return to the ship, leaving behind the parrot and the voyeur.

The days were heaven as we regressed to our childhood. We were going to our own homes. As we waved goodbye, I burst into unexpected tears.

AS PAUL HARVEY USED TO SAY
"AND NOW FOR THE REST OF THE STORY..."

When I reached my apartment, there was a message on my machine. I had taken someone else's luggage which was identical to mine. I was asked to return it to JFK the following day and exchange it for my own!

CHAPTER 51

2018 · Gyms & the Women in Them

As the music blares, 40 women place their equipment in the territory they claim for today. In any gym, the teacher is young, cute, and energetic. Women teach most categories, but the dance classes are almost always men, professional dancers and trainers.

Women teachers will have hair pulled back in a ponytail, no makeup, a perfect figure, and a cheerleader's attitude. That is the case in New York City. In my gym, in upstate New York, our teacher is a large, athletic woman, an Amazon without refinement. She is in great shape, but she spends the class talking about the beer hall she danced at last night.

I am not a gym rat, and I drag myself to keep my old bones from disintegrating and to keep my ability to move smoothly.

When I stand to begin class, I make sure I am in gear before I move. I lie on the floor at the end of class while everyone returns their mats. I move slowly to my knees to stand up. I use a large box under my head because I get vertigo and it helps. One day, I drank a large Coke before class. I didn't have the box, but I had two towels. As soon as I laid down flat, I threw up right into the two towels. It was only Coke, so it did not smell. No one noticed, and I quickly went to the ladies' room and got clean towels.

Before class, you grab two white towels, rough from bleach, detergent, and age. I pick up a rubber mat and I think the bacteria must be ferocious! The towels I take are for protection from the mat, used by everyone.

You can choose your spot and organize your equipment if you are early. In a conditioning class, you will use towels to make a circle for pulling and squeezing with both hands, torture blocks, and your water bottle. Stake out your territory. Squeeze into whatever space you can find, but don't walk away because someone else will take it.

The earlier crowd is usually the "in" group, and they converse before class. This group will not include you, no matter which gym you join. I am content to eavesdrop, but I learn nothing. These women could be models, dancers, acrobats, or stay-at-home moms dressed in fitted body tops, bare midriffs, and skin-tight exercise pants. The class ends with floor exercises and a cooldown. As I lie on the floor, always in the back row, I wonder if God will punish me for the unkind thoughts I have while critically evaluating the sizes and shapes in front of me.

People differ from gym to gym. Equinox on 63rd Street is the younger Upper East Side crowd. Designer outfits from Lulu Lemon are popular. Equinox has a wide variety of classes, and dance is high on the list at 10:00 each morning The teacher today is a young Latin man condensed into a 5'4" muscular body. He can leap and jump like a ballet dancer, making class fun as he cries out, "Show me some attitude!"

One woman dresses in a black baseball cap decorated with rhinestones. Her blonde ponytail is pulled through the back. She wears a scoop neck, sleeveless one-piece black bodysuit with a bit of an organza skirt tied around the waist. She is in superb condition in her late 60s and never without a secret smile as she watches herself in every mirror. The twenty-something instructor uses her to demonstrate steps with a partner.

One day, I brought my cousin Pattie, a fabulous dancer, as a guest. The instructor chose Pattie to illustrate the action, and Rhinestone-Hat almost lost it. The secret smile disappeared, and she missed several steps. On the way down the stairs after class, she bumped into Patti, almost knocking her over. An accident? I think not.

Yoga and Hot Pilates are a favorite at the Crunch gym. The room is about 90 degrees, and water and towels are necessary. Pilates stretches limbs and muscles. Yoga relaxes through deep breathing as you force your body into a plank position, pigeon position, and downward dog. You have to concentrate on your breathing, so there is no time for evaluating your class members.

Crunch is every man's gym. You can join by the month, and there is no attitude! It is clean and has plenty of lockers.

 Reebok, on the west side, is the studio for the stars. They attract the city's young professionals and have a colorful and staffed nursery for their privileged little offspring who may network in 30 years, remembering each other from the gym.

Reebok is also the gym for nudity. There is an executive locker room where you can leave your sweaty clothes, which will be washed, dried, and returned to your locker. Fax machines, copiers, and telephones are available for use. Cell phones are not allowed because they contain cameras.

The executive members are often pleasant. My daughter is a gym member and works one-on-one with a kickboxing instructor. After a session one night, she was kneeling in front of her locker gathering her things, and a woman behind her said, "You have a bad cough." My daughter started to say she had been in upstate New York, visiting her parents and caught a cold. She turned toward the speaker, who was naked and holding a towel over her arm, "I watched you kickboxing and would like to know about the instructor. He seemed fabulous," she said. Trying to keep her eyes on the woman's magnificently beautiful face, she managed the conversation with actress Kim Catrall.

Nudity in the locker room is nothing unusual. It is the lack of modesty that surprises me. Women shower at Reebok and Equinox, then wrap a towel around their waists and blow their hair dry in front of a mirror, breasts of all sizes bouncing to the music overhead. They sit on the benches with no panties, and I want to whip out my Clorox disinfectant wipes! However, the star of the show is still the woman who uses the blow dryer, carefully separating her buttocks to dry between them.

Needless to add, I dress and shower at home!

CHAPTER 52

1963–2007 · Walking Through a Time Warp: A College Student, a Young Wife, & a Grandmother

It has been snowing for the past few weeks, making the sidewalks slippery and the corners slushy with dirty, soot-blackened snow and small streams running around the corners looking for drains. These, too, are covered with little frozen hills. Nevertheless, I must go out and walk eight blocks to the Hospital for Special Surgery for my physical therapy appointments. I had a hip replacement and am still trying to strengthen the surrounding muscles.

I am afraid of falling, so I walk slowly and carefully. My mind drops through a time warp, and it is 1963. I turn left at the corner on First Avenue and start uptown. Instead of the storefronts, I am passing today, I go back in time and see those that were there in 1963, when I was a young wife of twenty-three, married to a medical student. This was my neighborhood. Here is the store, which was the Chinese laundry where I brought my sheets and where, two years later, Soo Lee would say, "You look so pregnant. When is the baby due?"

By what Chinese magic sight did she know that? I hadn't even seen the doctor yet to confirm it.

Across the street was M and J deli, where medical students, interns, and residents lined up for the giant sandwiches with a quarter pound of roast beef, lettuce, tomatoes, and mayo on rye, sandwiches the size of which you only find in New York City. My fiancé's group of unmarried students went there so often that they were on a first-name basis with Mitch and Jack, the M and J guys. One weekend, I brought a lasagna from my father's house on Long Island, where I was living, teaching first grade, and planning our wedding. The guys got M&J to bake it for them. I served it in the medical school dorm, which is still standing. The unmarried students lived in Olin Hall, where there were no kitchens. I wanted to impress our friends that I would be such a great wife.

Later, we would move next door into Livingston Farrand Apartments, where a studio was sixty-six dollars a month and about 450 square feet. I turn down Sixty-Ninth Street, past St. Catherine of Siena, where we attended mass every week for several years. I remember one spring morning when we had forgotten to turn our clocks ahead and attended eight o'clock mass instead of nine. We felt as if we had so much more day ahead of us that we would wake up the four unmarried guys still living in Olin Hall and go to Central Park. There are mountainous rocks on Seventieth Street inside the park near the playground, and those brilliant twenty-something fellows played Cowboys and Indians, hiding among the rocks and attacking each other.

Across the street from St. Catherine was our converted tenement, where we lived with other married students, each in a studio apartment. When they knocked it down last year to build a huge medical facility, we rescued a brick that will be the center of a collage of the years we lived there. One young genius, who has become a well-known TV medical news analyst, lived on the first floor. His doorway lined up with the front door. From his first-floor apartment, he could see any of us returning from the grocery store or work, carrying packages. As one leaned against the inside glass door, scrambling for the key buried deep in a purse or pocket, he would press the buzzer, making us lose balance and practically fall into the building.

The cellar of this building, which held washers and dryers, was dark and home to cockroaches as large as eggs. You could reach the back yard by walking through the dark basement at your own risk. Our husbands, who were students, decided to build a fountain in the back yard where we would sometimes cook out during the summer. They dug a hole and filled it with stones, using IV bottles and tubing to splash water. In the yard across a fence from ours, there were several men who also used their outdoor space. Every weekend in the summer, they could be seen in their wife-beater tee shirts, drinking beer together, and visiting. When it got too hot, they would rig up a hose out their kitchen windows to a shower head. They hung this on a clothesline using a pull chain to release the water and then stood under it to cool off. They called all the guys "Doc" because the third- and fourth year students wore white jackets to class with a shirt and tie.

I cross York Avenue and look back to a spot on the sidewalk where I can almost see our friend, Jack, throwing a baseball into the window of his fourth-floor dorm room. A homeless man on the corner yelled, "Did you see that kid? He threw the baseball right into the open window." Jack, who came from Iowa, had been a pitcher for Grinnell University. He is now the director of Breast Imaging at Brigham Women's Hospital in Boston and teaching his grandson, Jackson, to pitch.

One more block to HSS, the Hospital for Special Surgery, where our group often gathered for Sunday brunch. HSS had wonderful food in the cafeteria, and on Sunday, we would have chicken, mashed potatoes, carrots, cokes, and dessert for three dollars. I was still in college and visiting New York when we began to go there on weekends, and my friends were horrified.

"What do they serve … arms, legs, feet?" my friends asked.

George would regale us with his Saturday night exploits about town. He would later uncover a scandal within the Center for Disease Control and, eventually, become its director.

After physical therapy ends, I will walk home along York Avenue and remember that I used to cross the Avenue to avoid walking in front of Memorial Hospital, now called Memorial Sloan Kettering Cancer Center. I was afraid that a big hook would come out and pull me in. I didn't want to see cancer patients coming and going, so I would try to concentrate on the Rockefeller Institute and wonder what research was going on. I often prayed that I would never have to go inside that frightening building. Forty years later, I would run, not walk, to this building when I needed it.

On my next trip to therapy, I choose to cross at Sixty-Ninth Street and pass the front entrance to Weill Cornell Medical School. I will feel the sun, remembering the warm day in May 1965 when I carried my brand-new baby girl across York Avenue to her first home in our studio apartment. We did not know enough to get a taxi or car service. I had a "going home" outfit for her, a yellow bunting. It was too warm for a bunting, but I was determined to use it. She was jaundiced and matched the bunting in color. Three weeks later, our group would graduate, seventy men and four women, having earned the title of Medical Doctor.

Tomorrow, I will remember the third generation as I take a different route to HSS on Second Avenue, passing "Music and Me," where I took my grandson every Wednesday morning in 2002. We joined the other members of the class in singing Punchinello Happy Fellow. We learned about Aaron Copland, whose cowboy music was played as the class cantered in circles on their imaginary horses. On the way home, I will stop for a minute by Sokol Gym, where another generation of nannies, young mothers, and some grandmothers are packing children into strollers to go home for lunch. Remembering the games and songs my grandson and I learned there, I will walk the rest of the way home humming, *"The wheels on the bus go round and round, round and round, round and round. The wheels on the bus go round and round, all over town."*

CHAPTER 53

1977 · The Train

At midnight a train goes through Amsterdam on its way from Niagara Falls to New York City. I am about to fall asleep under downy quilts in our big bed. I wait to hear the low whistle. Amsterdam, my city now, is already asleep.

I had always lived in cities. I miss the sidewalks and the traffic lights. In the foothills of the Adirondacks all around us lies the Mohawk Valley with hayfields, rolling hills, and green trees. The Mohawk River winds its way from the great lakes to the Hudson River and the Statue of Liberty. My friends were always going to NY to see shows and museums. Everyone except me. My life was filled with children and horses.

On a typical weekend, we would bathe and braid the horses on Friday after school. At six in the morning on Saturday, we would drive the 800 feet to our barn and back our Wagoneer up almost perfectly. I roll the handle of the trailer down until it lands on the ball, tighten everything, and plug in the taillights. By now, the children had eaten and were dressed in their horse-show clothing. They had put in leaves of hay and sweet feed and had filled the water buckets last night. We put down the ramp, and Kim leads her big chestnut quarter horse in, hooks his halter and exits though the narrow door on the right. We call it the people door. Her horse, Diamond B. John, is so used to riding in the trailer that he could probably do it alone. Next, Chris would bring out Annie Buttons, a palomino angel of a horse, lock the trailer gate, and jump into the car. Just as it was getting light, we would drive off to seek horse-show friends and ribbons.

Our trainer is already there with stalls for us. He usually has about seven or eight of us at each show.

At our house, we have a pool and garden to keep up along with our horses, so summer flies by. During the long northeast winters, I often pretend that my house, which is all on one floor, is a penthouse apartment, and can see the hustle and bustle in a wave of nostalgia for New York City.

Many years later, when Kim is working and living in New York, Chris is in college. Eddie's sister, Helene, and her husband get transferred to the city with a dream apartment. We visited them often. Jimmy is always in the know, and he told us that prices were so low on apartments right now that the yuppies were getting rid of them cheaply, and we decided to look. People from his office are buying them as investments.

After six months of searching and upping our dollar amount, Kim called. She had gone to see an apartment I had found advertised for sale by owner. "You better get down here tomorrow," she said, "I think this is it." We had searched together so often that some of the doormen thought that I was the broker, and the apartment was for Kim and Eddie. It is not unusual to see older men with young wives in Manhattan.

On my 50th birthday at 11:45 p.m., Kim and I struggled with the lock to get into our new apartment while it was still my birthday. There was one king-sized bed we both slept in it, and Con Ed had turned on the electricity in our name. There was a full bathroom, and a kitchen with no food.

It was a dream come true. I like the country and all its beauty, but I LOVE THE CITY!

I am in my apartment about 70 days of each year, alone or with Kim, who lives there, and sometimes Eddie. The train takes three hours and it is a beautiful ride along the river until it crawls into the darkness of Grand Central. The passengers go into action, pulling luggage from the top rack. I jump off quickly and take the F train uptown and when I am in the apartment, I pinch myself. I pick up the phone and order a piece of seven-layer chocolate cake and a coke, which is delivered in ten minutes. Bloomingdales is three blocks away, and the Metropolitan Museum of Art is a twenty-minute walk along fifth Avenue. I wear black all the time because everyone does. I don't care if it snows. The subway and the buses run all the time.

Famous people sit across from you, and you smile at them. Meg Ryan walks past with her hair looking like she did it with an eggbeater. Julia Roberts hails a cab, and her smile lights up Second Avenue. We walk up Madison, and I say (louder than I thought,) "Oh my, here is Dominik Dunne." He hears me and stops to say hello.

Sadly, Jimmy and Helene move back to Michigan, and we miss them terribly. However, we have made wonderful new friends with an endodontist, Sam, and his wife, Anne, who is from Ireland. They have introduced us to their friends Kathy and Ron, and their children are all in middle school and treat us like family.

We think will see them go to college, have several happy and sad relationships, find the right person, and marry in ten years — and we do!

Whenever we return home from a few days' visit, we are exhausted from the New York pace. When I am home again, falling asleep, I'll hear the whistle blow as the train leaves the station, but I know it will come back for me when I need it.